GW00671514

THE MESSAGE TO THE CHURCH
Isabel Chapman

Isabel Chapman

ISBN 978-184426-482-7

First Published 2008 by.
UPFRONT PUBLISHING LTD
Peterborough, England.

Printed by Lightning Source

Isabel Chapman

Dedication

I dedicate this book to the body of Christ in all nations, tribes, and language. This is our day. Like the first century saints we must earnestly contend for the faith once delivered unto the saints. Like the first century saints, the body of Christ in our generation has been commissioned to obey the Lord's command.

"Go into all the world and preach the gospel to every creature.

He that believes and is baptized shall be saved; but he that believes not shall be damned.

And these signs shall follow those who believe; in my name they shall cast out devils; they shall speak with new tongues;

They shall take up serpents; and if they drink any deadly thing it shall not hurt them; they shall lay hands on the sick and they shall recover.

So then after the Lord had spoken unto them, he was received up into heaven, and sat on the right hand of God.

And they went forth, and preached everywhere, the Lord working with them, and confirming his word with signs following." (Mark 16: 15-20)

The purpose of this book is to encourage the body of Christ to obey the great commission, and expect God to work with us confirming the preaching of the gospel with signs following.

Isabel Chapman

Acknowledgments

My meeting with Pastors Eduardo and Marilyn Padua was by divine appointment. They worked along side me during my mission to the head hunting people of Kalinga Apayao. Since 1980 they have continued to oversee the work in the remote areas, as well as oversee the mission in Cabaroan in my absence. I would like to express my gratitude for their faithfulness and commitment to Christ and their love and care for His sheep.

To Elizabeth West and Ruth Woodhouse who painstakingly worked on the proof reading of this book. Thank you dear sisters for your labour of love in the Lord's service, which is greatly appreciated.

Isabel Chapman

Preface

With this book Isabel attempts to bring to our notice some glaring theological omissions and errors of our Christian faith. Essential tenets of our faith that have been known in previous generations have been allowed to slip into disuse, and forgotten in this generation. We are therefore in a hybrid state of thinking we are Christians, but in fact we only understand a half-gospel and not the full gospel.

Consequently the great commission to "teach, preach, heal, cast out demons and raise the dead" seems a far-fetched idea and an impossible command. However the gospel contained in this book will explain why we fail to implement our Lord's commission – and more importantly show us how to fulfil our Lord's command.

Those of us who have been searching for the key to a healing ministry like our Lord's, will be amazed at the simplicity of the unravelled mystery. Isabel distinguishes between religion or religious observance, and faith in the word of God. She illustrates with examples from her own experience how God the Father acts when the true gospel is preached. As God has spoken – so should we expect – or conclude that God is a liar.

His truth in this book will set the captives free – not our version of the truth – but the version set down in the gospels and early letters. The essential first version that set the known world ablaze. I trust that you will read, mark and inwardly digest this urgent letter to the church.

If we want a vibrant church, we must preach a vibrant gospel.

This book shows us a living Lord who keeps His promises in every way.

Ruth Woodhouse
Methodist Local Preacher

THE MESSAGE TO THE CHURCH
Isabel Chapman

Isabel Chapman

Chapter One

Botany Bay is situated on the North East coast of Scotland where my earliest memories lie.We lived in a little three-roomed house only a stones throw away from the sand dunes and expanse of beautiful golden sands, where the North Sea pounded the seashore with every high tide. Electricity and running water were foreign to us. Our only means of light was a lamp, which gave light by means of a wick steeped in paraffin. A well which was merely a hole in the ground, supplied us with water that was carried in buckets back to our little house. The pathway between the house and our well was a well beaten little track. Water had to be carried for drinking, cooking, cleaning and washing.

It never entered our thinking that the water could have been contaminated, as it was also used by all the wild life in the surrounding area. It was the breeding ground for the local frogs and toads. In the spawning season we had to move the eggs to one side to immerse the bucket in the water. As the tadpoles began to grow legs and swim freely around the surface of the well, they got caught in the bucket and were carried home. Then we had the fun of carefully catching them in a ladle, and placing them in a soup bowl, in order to carry them safely back to their natural habitat. My playground was the sand dunes and sea shore. The golden sands sparkled and glittered as if mingled with minute little diamonds when the summer sun was high in the sky.

The towering sand dunes were a wonderful play park and my great joy. I would scramble up the narrow tracks which zigzagged between the sharp pointed grasses that grew on the banks of the barren sand hills. Higher and higher I clambered, usually ending up crawling on all fours as I reached the summit. All along the coastline stood a range of sand dunes that formed a wall of defence, which sheltered the neighbouring farm cottages from the cold blasts of North Sea winter gales. On the pinnacle of the highest dune, I would look over the great expanse of water which stretched as far as the eye could see. Even when the sun was shining, standing on top of the various pinnacles, one had to face the biting cold North Sea wind. On occasions it threatened to take my breath away, as it whipped at my cheeks and tore at my hair and clothes and threatened to topple me over. To escape the biting wind I would find a hollow between the sand dunes, where I would take refuge and shelter, and stretch out on the sand and enjoy the warmth of the sun in my secluded sunken little hiding place. Having soaked in the warmth of the sun, I would retrace my steps to the top of the highest dune. Throwing myself down in total abandonment, I would roll from the summit to the base. The experience was exhilarating, as well as a little frightening, as there was no stopping mid way. As the speed increased at the steepest point of the dune, there was only one way to go - down. There was no stopping until I came to a halt at the base of the great mountain of golden sand. There I would lie on my back on the sea shore and listen to the sound of the sea, which had different voices. Sometimes it sounded kind, gentle and friendly as it lapped around the rocks, at other times it sounded harsh, angry and unfriendly when the enormous waves constantly pounded down and beat upon the rocks and the little sea creatures which lived in the rock pools.

When the voice of the sea sounded kind, gentle and

friendly, I enjoyed exploring God's amazing creation of little sea creatures. As an inquisitive child, I was fascinated by the many different species which lived in the pools and clung to the rocks. The brightly coloured sea anemones with their waving tentacles were my favourites. At high tide when the big waves rolled in and crashed on the seashore with deafening, thundering crashes the voice of the sea sounded harsh, angry and unfriendly, as if sounding an alarm of danger. I would sit leaning against my favourite sand dune, wondering how all the little creatures, especially the fragile sea anemones, could possibly survive under the power and force of those enormous waves. Wandering along the sea shore, it seemed as though nothing else in the whole wide world existed except the endless stretch of sandy beach and great expanse of water. As far as the eye could see the golden sands stretched out like a great expanse of shimmering desert, which seemed to dance and sparkle as the rays of the sun glinted on little particles of broken and crushed shells.

Nothing green grew along the sea shore, nothing lived there, not even a single shrub or tree, yet the place had a unique tranquil beauty which filled my soul with peace and joy. Occasionally I found pieces of broken driftwood, which were fashioned into curious shapes and designs and tangled up with brown shriveled seaweed. There were lots shells to be found along the deserted beach. When I held one to my ear I could hear the voice of the sea resounding within the shell. This realy puzzled me. I was always conscious of the seagulls wheeling around and overhead, and calling out as if giving instructions to one another. The sand crabs were difficult to see and loved to play hide-and-seek. When they heard the sound of approaching feet they scuttled away and disappeared into their burrows, leaving pretty circular designs in the sand. Sometimes I lay down flat on my stomach, hardly daring to breathe, waiting for the crabs to reappear, but somehow they knew I was there, and remained hidden until I was long gone.

At low tide, when the voice of the sea sounded gentle and inviting, I became totally absorbed clambering over and round the rocks. I investigated the rock pools, looking to see if the little creatures, and especially the brightly coloured sea anemones, had survived under the power and weight of the gigantic high tide waves. Excitedly I clambered over the rocks, wanting to know if the anemones, little crabs and sea creatures were still alive, or if they had been smashed to smithereens against the rocks. It was a miracle. They were still in the same little rock pools and the anemones were still waving their tentacles as if praising the Lord for their divine protection. I came to the conclusion that God, who created the little sea creatures, protected and sheltered them from the power and force of those pounding waves. God was revealing Himself to me through His amazing creation. I did not know God, but I could sense Him, and feel His awesome presence, in the wonder of the amazing unfathomable beauty of nature which surrounded me at Botany Bay. There was a desire growing in me to truly know God. He had not only created the beauty of nature in which I was blessed to live, but He had also created me a unique individual for His praise and glory.

At five years of age my mother enrolled me at Crimond Primary School. Although it was the nearest school, it felt as though it was at the other side of the world. I walked through the fields to take a short cut to the road, which ended at what we called the Lighthouse buildings, where the Lighthouse workers and their families lived. Heading down the road in the opposite direction from the Lighthouse buildings, I could see the Loch of Strathbeg. It was a beautiful picture in the summer months when the sun was shining, but a very different picture in winter time. In the winter months the scene was cold, grey and foreboding and sent cold shivers up my spine.

As I reached the bottom of the hill, I could look up to my right and see the homes of the Coastguard workers and their families. The Coastguard workers were brave men who were called out to sea if there was a ship in distress. To save men's lives they had to face the power and force of the gigantic North Sea waves, as well as the fierce gale force winds. As I walked towards the farm I meditated on the way that God sheltered and protected the sea anemones under the power and force of every high tide. It was then that I prayed my first prayer to God, who was drawing me to Himself by His amazing grace. "God, please shelter and protect the Coastguard men when they have to go to sea to save the fishermen, in the same way as you keep the little sea creatures and anemones safe under your divine protection every high tide." My walk ended at the farmhouse where the school bus picked us up. The road from the Light House buildings to the farm was only a single track, which widened into a two way road at the farm. The walk to and from home to the farmhouse took approximately thirty minutes each way. In the winter months I had to face the freezing cold North winds, blizzards and cold damp fog. Sometimes the fog was so thick that one could only see a yard ahead. At such times the foghorn sounded continuously to warn the ships that they were getting close to the shore. If they got too close they would end up grounded on the hazardous rocks.

My walk home from the farm was a joy in the summertime when the sun was shining and the air lovely and warm. At a certain point I would leave the lighthouse children and take a short cut through the fields. I enjoyed the peace and tranquility of the surrounding views. In front of me stood the wall of picturesque sand dunes of various sizes and shapes. Behind was the endless expanse of sea and the white lighthouse standing tall and erect, towering out of the midst of the water, which shone and dazzled against the background of the dark blue sea. Sitting down in the grassy field to rest, I drank in the scenic beauty which surrounded me on all sides, and picked the daisies around me to make a daisy chain necklace. The air was warm, quiet and peaceful, except for the sound of an occasional bleating lamb, or the screeching of the lapwings and terns calling overhead. As I chained the daisies together I kept an eye on the lapwings rising from their nests built on the grassy field. I made a mental note of where the lapwings rose from their nesting places. I then went to look for the nests, and count the number of eggs in each nest. It was a sheer joy to see another egg added every day, until the standard number of four or five eggs was neatly arranged in each nest. Then I played the waiting game, and guessed which nest would produce the first chicks. It was amazing and exciting to see the eggs produce scrawny, helpless little chicks, and see them with their little yellow beaks gaping wide open waiting to be fed.

Getting off the school bus one beautiful summer day Jimmy, who was double my age and the son of one of the Light House keepers, unexpectedly came and walked along the road by my side.

He asked, "Do you know where the lapwings nest in the fields where you take your short cut home?"

I replied, "Yes, I know where thirteen nests are situated and there are sixty two chicks altogether."

"Will you show them to me?" he asked.

"No! They are my secret." I replied.

"Come on. Don't be a spoil sport. I will carry the

paraffin for you if you show me."

I had to bring the paraffin home for our lamp. I bought it from the garage where the school bus dropped us, near to the school. On our route home the bus stopped to drop off my cousins, and auntie Betty handed me two pints of milk in a carrier bag, which I also had to carry home. Living in what the locals called 'the back of beyond' it was not worth the milkman's time or trouble to deliver milk to such an out of the way place. It was a heavy load for a five-year-old to carry. I had my schoolbag on my back, a gallon can of paraffin in one hand, and two pints of milk in the other. To relieve myself from carrying the weight of the can of paraffin, I agreed to let Jimmy come with me on my short cut, and show him where the lapwing nests were situated. At the gate where I left the other children to take my short cut, I slipped the bag containing the two bottles of milk through the barbed wire, and placed them on the other side of the fence, and did the same with the gallon of paraffin. I then climbed up and over the gate and down the other side, with Jimmy following my lead. Picking up the milk and handing the paraffin to Jimmy, I headed towards the first lapwing nest, which housed five little chicks. The chicks were at that point four days old and beginning to grow their first downy feathers. Kneeling down by the nest I said, "Look Jimmy, the chicks are so cute and sweet. They are always hungry with their little yellow beaks wide open waiting for their mummy to come and feed them." Then his tone of voice startled me and sent shivers of fear running up and down my spine. He was mocking me by repeating what I had said in a horrible voice, ending with the words, "You girls are just stupid gutless sissies. What is cute and sweet about scrawny birds with gaping beaks? This is what I think about the stupid looking things." I was shocked, stunned, hurt and alarmed by his words, and his following actions were beyond my comprehension. I had never before encountered the kind of evil that was in his heart. From my kneeling position by the nest, I stared up at him with horrified eyes. I simply could not believe that any individual would want to hurt the helpless little chicks. I saw his right hand go into his right pocket. At that precise moment there was a screeching noise above our heads and the mother lapwing "dive bombed" Jimmy. His reaction was to raise his hand above his head as a form of defence.

I had knelt by every nest, and had spoken to the chicks on my way home from school every day since they hatched, but the parent birds had never once "dive bombed" me. I came to the quick conclusion that the parent birds knew their chicks were in danger. Then it happened again, the screeching noise of two lapwings above our heads, and both birds "dive bombed" Jimmy in an attempt to protect their young. He bent down and picked up a stone and threw it into the air saying, "You dumb stupid birds. You cannot frighten me." His hand went into his right pocket for the second time and he brought out a penknife. As quick as a flash he opened the blade, knelt down picked a chick out of the nest, and cut off its little head. "No, that is an evil thing to do." I screamed as I threw myself at him in an attempt to try and stop him. He threw me to the ground. He pinned me down with his knee on my chest, I could feel the blade of the penknife touching my neck. He spat in my face and said, "If you attack me again, I will stick this blade into your neck." I lay on my back too stunned and terrified to move, but turned my head to see what he was doing, then immediately shut my eyes because the scene was so ghastly, horrendous, and murderous. He was taking great pleasure in beheading every little chick in the nest.

I cried out, "Help me, God", then I was on my feet running as fast as my feet would carry me in the direction of my home. He caught up with me, and yelled into my face, "Show me where the other nests are." My heart stopped racing, my knees stopped shaking, fear left me and an uncanny, unexplainable peace flooded my being. I was amazed by the fearless boldness that had come over me, and replied, "Even if you stick your knife into my throat, I will never, never, never tell you where to find another nest." Righteous anger rose in me and I screamed, "You are a murderer. You have killed five helpless little baby chicks." My hair was long, almost down to my waist, and neatly braided in one big plait, which hung down my back. He grabbed my plait and violently dragged me by my hair in the direction of a big clump of stinging nettles. He let go of my plait and put his two hands around my neck and squeezed as he said, "If you tell anyone about this, your punishment will be far worse than I am giving you now." He picked me up bodily and threw me into the center of the clump of stinging nettles, and walked away laughing.

The nettles stung me every time I moved. From brow to ankle, my body was on fire with stinging pain. Every sting caused a white lump to appear on my skin. I was in torment with the pain, stung through my school blouse and covered all over with white lumps. I did not know what to do with myself and started jumping up and down screaming out in agony. The thought came to my mind, "Find the dock leaf. The sap will relieve the pain." The dock leaf grew in marshy areas, so I headed towards the pond at top of the hill where the shepherd watered the sheep. Every step was agony, but I was suddenly there, and I wildly pulled a dock leaf, broke the stem and started to rub my hands and arms with the sap. I pulled another, broke the stem and rubbed my ears and all over my face and neck, and continued the procedure over and over again until every sting was treated by the sap of the dock leaf.

Slowly but surely the pain began to subside. The events of the past minutes had been so traumatic, and painful that I collapsed and fell into a deep sleep lying by the side of the pond.

I awoke just before dark and my body was at peace. The stinging had ceased and the white lumps were beginning to disappear. I was going to be in trouble for being late home from school. I remembered that the milk and paraffin were by the nest of the murdered chicks. Running with all my strength back to where the most horrific event of my life had happened, I knelt at the nest and spoke to the parents of the dead chicks. "Please forgive me. It is all my fault that your babies are dead, I should not have told that evil Jimmy where to find your nest." I looked up, because I heard the familiar call of the lapwings, and saw the parent birds circling above me. Then one took the lead and the other fell in behind heading in the direction of my home. My schoolbag was still on my back, which had saved the top part of my back from getting stung. Picking up the can of paraffin and the carrier bag with the two bottles of milk I headed down the hill. Looking above, I could see the parent lapwings flying in unison leading the way, then they gave me their usual shrill call, veered to the left and off they flew. I was forgiven, and God would enable them to make more eggs which would produce new babies.

Then I heard my mother's voice crying out in worried desperation as I neared our garden gate, "Where have you been? I was beginning to think that the school bus must have had an accident, or had broken down." It was then that I told my first lie. "I tripped and fell into the clump of stinging nettles and was stung all over, so I went back to the pond and rubbed myself with the sap of the dock leaf. When the stinging stopped I was so relieved that I fell asleep."

"What on earth were you doing beside the clump of stinging nettles?"

"I was looking for another lapwing's nest." As I passed her by and headed for the kitchen to relieve myself of the weight of the milk and paraffin, I was pricked in my conscience that I had told my second lie through fear of Jimmy's threat. Walking in behind me Mother took my left hand and ran her hand over the flesh of my arm, and felt the lumps in my skin. "One sting from a stinging nettle is very painful. To be stung all over must have been like a terrible nightmare. Thank God you had the sense to treat yourself with the sap from the dock leaf," she said, giving me a reassuring hug.

The following morning, as I reached the top of the hill on my way to meet the school bus, my heart missed a beat, when I saw the solitary figure of Jimmy waiting at the gate for me. Panic grabbed me and I reacted in fear and wanted to turn around and run home as fast as my feet would carry me. Then that unexplainable peace and calm that I had experienced the day before came over me, and I fearlessly walked on. Approaching the gate I shouted to him, "Why are you standing there waiting for me?" Climbing up the gate, I sat perched on the top bar looking down at him waiting for his answer. He did not answer my question, but instead asked me a question. "Did you tell your mother?"

"No, I told her I was looking for a lapwing's nest and tripped and fell into the nettles. If you ever speak to me again, I will tell my father when he comes home, and he will go and tell your father, and they will both throw you into the clump of stinging nettles, and they will not allow you to use the dock leaf for relief. I mean what I say!"

He took off, and began to run along the road in front of me. He never did speak to me again. A week later his father was promoted and they moved away to another district, much to my relief.

On my way home through the fields, I often met the shepherd on his evening round as he worked with his dog to gather in the sheep for the final count of the day. The sheep all looked alike to me, but the shepherd told me that each sheep had its own special identity, character and personality. He knew his sheep, and could identify each individual one. "But they look identical. How can you tell one from another?"

"A shepherd knows his own sheep." was his reply.

"What do you think about school, young lady?" he asked me on that occasion. I furrowed my eyebrows, shook my head and walked on, hoping that my expression would reveal my answer. As I walked on, I could hear the sound of his hearty laugh behind me. I did not like school. My preference was to stay at home and feel God's presence by the sea shore whilst exploring the rocks and pools, or being in the fields counting the number of different species of wild flowers, daisies, buttercups, bluebells and little pansies with their beautifully painted delicate faces. Or flitting through the fields following the butterflies, as they gracefully fluttered from flower to flower. I enjoyed sitting watching the lapwing chicks attempt to take their first flight. There was never a dull moment, there was always something new to see and experience. God's amazing creation was always full of wonderful surprises.

However, I grew to accept the fact that it did not matter how much I complained about not wanting to go to school. It could not be avoided. So I decided to make the best of a bad deal and stop complaining, which rather irritated my mother. By the time I reached primary three, school had taken on a new interest for me. Our music teacher wrote the 23rd Psalm on the blackboard, and we had to copy it out, and then memorize it. When the entire class could recite it from memory, our teacher sat on the piano stool and began to play a tune, and sing the words of the 23rd Psalm to the tune. It sounded so beautiful, and I cried because I felt God's presence for the first time in school.

Mrs. Ingram explained the history of the tune, which was composed by the minister's daughter of our local church a few centuries ago. She named the tune, "Crimond" which was the name of our village, and the place where she and we were born. "The Lord is My Shepherd" to the tune Crimond, became very famous and is still sung in many churches throughout Europe. It was a great joy for me to learn to sing the psalm to the tune Crimond, and I accepted Jesus as my Shepherd, and my heart overflowed with love for Him. On my shortcut through the fields on my way home from school I would sing, "The Lord is My Shepherd" to the tune Crimond, with all my heart, in full voice.

On one such occasion Jesus revealed Himself to me in such a wonderful way. It was so real and true, that it has lived with me to this very day, some fifty years later. With arms raised heavenward singing, "The Lord is my shepherd, I shall not want" in full voice, and heart pounding with love and gratitude for having such a loving caring Shepherd to watch over me, the scene changed. The field where I was standing turned into an indescribably beautiful meadow. The grass was greener and lusher than can be explained and strewn with the most beautiful flowers, of many and varied vivid colors. The beauty was exquisite and not of this world. Then a figure appeared dressed in brilliant white. I could not see His face for the glory and brilliance that surrounded Him. Then He held out His arms, and I ran as fast as I could into those outstretched arms. He caught me in His hands, threw me into the air, and caught me again, holding me above his head with outstretched arms. Jesus

13

said, "You are mine. You belong to me."

Then I was back standing in the familiar field, which looked so drab, and dull and dead compared to the exquisite beauty I had just seen. I do not know if it was a vision or if my spirit was caught up to the heaven. All I know is that it happened as explained. I knew that my Shepherd knew me as a unique individual sheep. I also knew that He had accepted me as a sheep of His pasture. I belonged to Him. Joy and happiness overwhelmed me, and I danced around the field giving praise and thanksgiving to my Shepherd singing, "I am yours and you are mine. I belong to you." I was such a precious experience that I kept it a guarded secret throughout my growing years.

Soon afterwards my mother announced that we were moving house. She had applied for one of the new houses on the newly built council estate at Crimond. She was one of the first to be granted a new home, because of the poor sanitary conditions in which we lived at Botany Bay. Of course she was thrilled and overjoyed. It meant that she would not spend half of each day fetching water from the well. No more smelly paraffin lamps to fill, no more dry toilet pails to empty into a hole in the ground. She would have electricity, tapped water and a hygienic toilet for the first time in her life. I was glad for my mother, but the thought of leaving Botany Bay where I got to know God's peace and presence filled me with gloom and sadness. I tried not to show my true feelings, and tried to sound enthusiastic and pleased. But Mother discerned that I was not happy about the move, and proceeded to tell me about all the new benefits I would be able to enjoy. We would even get a television. However, nothing she said changed my inner feeling of losing my most precious possession, God's peace and presence that reigned at Botany Bay.

Chapter Two

Our house contents were packed in cardboard boxes of varying sizes, and littered the floor of the main room which led to the one and only door of the little house which I loved so much. This would be the last night I would go to sleep listening to the sound of the waves crashing on the sea shore, thinking of God protecting and sheltering the sea anemones, and all His little sea creatures which lay beneath the might and power of the high tide mountainous waves. I did not want to leave, and was trying so hard not to cry, but the lump in my throat was becoming unbearable as I wandered around the room in a daze, not wanting to believe what was actually happening.

Mother and my two little sisters were busy in the bedroom packing the last box. They were so happy, as Father was due home within the hour. He had managed to get time off work to come home and help Mother with the move. Suddenly my eyes fixed on an envelope lying on the table. The words "Birth Certificates" were written in Mother's handwriting. It was not sealed so I opened it and saw my birth certificate for the first time. As I read I was stunned, shocked and thrown into a state of confusion. I was registered and known in school with the surname Summers, yet my birth certificate read: Fathers name, Alfred Chapman. My knees shook to the extent that I could no longer stand and I sank to the floor, at the precise moment the door opened and father shouted, "I am home!" With shouts of joy mother and my little sisters appeared from the bedroom and warm embraces were exchanged all round, as I hid myself under the table. No one seemed to notice that I was not present. In my hiding place under the table despair and rejection gripped my heart. I did not belong. The man I believed to be my father was not my father, and the man who was my father was a total stranger.

My baby sister needed some attention and Mother shouted, "Isabel, where are you? Eileen needs her nappy changed." Then she turned to her husband and said, "I can't understand her, from the day I told her that we are moving to our new house in Crimond, she has changed, she has become silent and withdrawn. I do not know what is going on in her head. She goes about singing or humming the hymn about the Lord being her Shepherd."

Hearing those words reminded me that I belonged to my Shepherd. Sitting in my hiding place under the table hidden by all the packed boxes, the voice of my Shepherd spoke from somewhere inside me and said, "I will never leave you nor forsake you." Then I realized that I was still holding my birth certificate in my hand. The devastation, hurt, rejection that reading the document had caused me was gone. I was not hurting any more, I had all the assurance that I needed, my Shepherd would never leave me or forsake me. I crawled out from under the table and stood on my feet, and handed my birth certificate to my mother. Our eyes met in a knowing look, and I took my two little sisters to our bedroom. The emotional trauma of the day had taken its toll on me as an eight-year-old child. But the voice of my Shepherd stilled my pounding heart and brought me comfort and peace. I soon drifted into sleep, listening to the sound of the waves pounding on the seashore.

I awoke to the skirl of seagulls heading towards the sea. Dread filled my heart. This was the day we were moving house. The farmer arrived with his tractor and trailer soon after eight o'clock in the morning, and all hands were on deck as every one helped to load boxes and furniture onto the trailer. I was the only one who cried as we were driven away. I felt cut off from my Shepherd. The rest of the family thought it was the best thing that could have happened to them. My birth certificate was not mentioned throughout the course of the day or for many years thereafter. Everyone was so preoccupied and excited about the move to the new house. It was a nice house with three bedrooms and a bathroom upstairs and a big lounge and kitchen downstairs. We could actually see the sea and the Loch of Strathbeg from the front bedroom window.

Within a week the house was in perfect order and everything in its rightful place. Father went back to his usual work routine, which meant he came home for a long weekend at the end of each month, and we settled down to life at Crimond. Mother was not interested and did not want to attend the local church, but my sisters and I went with the other children in the village to attend Sunday School. The minister informed our mother that she should give her consent for her three daughters to be baptized into the Church of Scotland and become members of the Church family. Dressed in her Sunday best Mother attended church for the first time, and we, her three daughters, were duly baptized by water sprinkling. Then the minister said a prayer, and with his thumb marked the imprint of a cross in our foreheads. This signified that we were now Church family and belonged to the Church of Scotland. I remembered the voice of my Shepherd saying, "You are mine. You belong to me." I became convinced that God lived at Botany Bay and that I would never feel His peace and presence in my new location.

I was soon to find out that God was not restricted to living at Botany Bay. A mission from a nearby town came to our village and held their meetings in the village hall. As soon as I entered the building God's peace flooded my being, and I cried out, "God, you are here!" The one in charge of the mission heard my cry and said to me,

"How do you know God is here?"

"I can feel His peace!" was my reply.

"Do you know God?" he asked.

"Yes, He is my Shepherd and I belong to Him!"

"It is truly wonderful that you have this conviction of belonging to God at such a young age. How did it happen?"

"That is my secret!"

At that point a lady started to strum on a guitar and sing: "I am redeemed. I am redeemed, by the blood of the Lamb, by the blood of the Lamb.

"I am redeemed by the blood of the Lamb, filled with the Holy Ghost, I am.

"All my sins are under the blood. I've been redeemed."

We were given paper and a pencil and were told to write down the song, and then we were told every one who could recite the song by memory the following evening would receive a prize. As I memorized the song that evening in my bed, I spoke to God and said, "What does redeemed mean?" The voice of my Shepherd spoke inside me and said, "You will know tomorrow." I was thrilled, overjoyed and began to realize that God was everywhere. He is at Botany Bay, He is in the village hall, now He is in my bedroom. The thought that God was in my bedroom filled me with unspeakable joy. As I snuggled down beneath the warmth of my bedclothes, the voice of my Shepherd said, "I am in you." I sat bolt upright in bed and said, "God, how can you be in me?"

"You will know tomorrow. Sleep now." Snuggling back down again I went to sleep knowing God's perfect peace again.

The following day dragged past. I felt it was the longest

day of my life, and could hardly contain myself, being full of expectation about what I was going to learn in the mission meeting. I was the first one there, and waited by the hall door for the mission team to arrive. Then the caretaker arrived, and opened the doors and I followed him inside and watched him turn on the lights. The question was bursting inside me, and I blurted out, "Is God inside you?"

"That is a strange thing to ask." he said, as he stood in front of me scratching his head. I could see that he was applying great thought to my question, and I did not dare break into his thinking. Finally he spoke, "No, God is not inside me, I have too many bad habits and sins for God to be in me." With that he hurried out of the building and left me standing there on my own meditating on his answer. The mission team arrived and I immediately went to Peter, who had spoken to me the previous evening. "Peter, is God inside you?" He did not hesitate as the caretaker had done and immediately said, "Yes, the Holy Spirit lives in me. My body is God's house. Is God inside you?"

"Yes"

"How do you know that God is inside you?" asked Peter.

"God speaks to me from inside me, and He told me that He is inside me."

"Do you know when God came inside you?"

I had to think hard to answer that question, then the words came to me, "When I was in Primary Three we had to memorize the 23rd psalm and I knew and accepted Jesus as my Shepherd. That was when Jesus came inside me."

Peter went on to explain that it is the Spirit of Jesus that comes to live in us, and that Jesus is in heaven at the right hand of the Father, forever praying and interceding for us. I then understood that it was the Holy Spirit that lived in me

19

and talked to me.

"What does redeemed mean?"

"You will learn about that in the lesson this evening."

By the end of the meeting I understood the meaning of redeemed: bought back and set free from punishment for sin. I also understood that Jesus' death and blood was the ransom payment that cancelled out all our sins. Jesus was the sinless Lamb of God who willingly gave His life, to pay the full payment for the sins of the world, to save believers from the second death, in the terrible place called the lake of fire and brimstone. All the children in the meeting could sing the chorus with full understanding and faith:

I am redeemed. I am redeemed, by the blood of the Lamb, by the blood of the Lamb.

I am redeemed by the blood of the lamb, filled with the Holy Ghost, I am.

All my sins are under the blood. I've been redeemed.

God's grace grants repentance to those who believe and accept Jesus as their sin bearer and Redeemer. There was great rejoicing in heaven that night when approximately fifty children were regenerated by the power of the indwelling Holy Ghost. I felt so sorry for the caretaker, who did not understand that Jesus' death had paid the full penalty for all his sins, and decided that I must tell him the good news. So I was at the hall door waiting for him to come and open up the following evening. I waited patiently until he had done the necessary and switched on the lights before attempting to talk to him. Before I had a chance to speak, he turned to me and said, "Is there any hope that God would come inside me?"

"Yes, because your sins have already been forgiven. Jesus' death and blood paid the ransom price for the sins of everybody in the whole world."

"How do you know that is true?"

"It is written in the Bible. Wait and talk to Peter and he will tell you, and convince you by reading the scriptures to you."

Peter witnessed to the caretaker and read the relevant scriptures to him. He believed, and received his forgiveness by faith in God's word, and God the Holy Spirit took up residence within him. I knew it had happened to him because of the peace and joy in his face. He stayed on to attend the meetings each evening and grew in the knowledge of God. It was a wonderful week's mission and we knew without doubt or shadow that, "God is good all the time."

After the mission left I started to attend a fellowship with my cousin Isabel and her family in Peterhead. I loved being with the sheep who knew Jesus as their personal Shepherd. However, a gap was widening between my parents and me. I could not help singing praises to God. He was in me, and I was in Him, and I could not hide the joy of the Lord that bubbled up out of me. I was told on many occasions, "Shut your mouth. We are fed up hearing about the blood of Jesus Christ."

One day I retaliated and said, "If you knew the value of the blood of Jesus, you would not talk like that."

That earned me a sharp slap across the face, and my mother said, "Your father says that you have religious mania. We will not allow you to go to these religious meetings anymore."

"He is not my father, so he cannot stop me going to the meetings. God in heaven is my Father, Jesus is my Shepherd, and the Holy Ghost lives in me"

My step-father turned to my mother and said, "That religion has turned her brain. She is talking nonsense." He grabbed me by the shoulders and yelled into my face, "As long as you are under my roof and provision, you will do as

I tell you."

In desperation I decided to run away. Waiting till the house was silent and everyone was fast asleep, I crept past my parents' bedroom door with pounding heart, and tiptoed down the stairs noiselessly. With shaking hands and knees, I opened the front door and stepped out into the darkness.

Chapter Three

Running as fast as my legs could carry me I headed up the road and came to a breathless halt by the local phone box. A thought entered my mind, "Ring your cousin Isabel, and ask her to come and get you." Lifting the receiver I dialed the operator and asked her to place a reverse charge call, which my cousin accepted, and I tearfully explained to her my dilemma. She told me to go back home and go to bed so that my parents would not know that I had left the house. "Why can you not come and take me home to be with you?"

"Because you are under age and your parents will not approve."

"He is not my father, God is my Father." I protested.

"Your parents are not saved. They do not understand. Please go back home and go to bed."

As a ten-year-old child I did not understand the implication of my cousin's words. Replacing the receiver I felt totally rejected by one whom I knew to be a sheep of Christ's pasture. No! I would not go back to that house where the value of my Shepherds blood was mocked and His name used as a swearword. I should have spoken to my Shepherd and waited to hear His voice, but my carnal feelings were ruling me and I felt hurt, rejected, helpless and downcast. Where could I go?

Looking around me I realized that I was out on my own, all alone in the middle of the night. In the heavens above the moon was shining giving light and the sky was full of twinkling stars. Then I remembered the words of my Shepherd, "I will never leave you or forsake you." There was no need for me to be afraid. God was with me, even in me. The headlights of an approaching car made me get back into the phone box, crouch down and hide. I did not want anyone to see me out alone in the dark of night. Sitting in that crouched position, waiting for the car to pass by, I decided to head for my beloved Botany Bay and rest in God's peace and presence. It was approximately six miles away. It was a busy main road. In order not to be seen by passing traffic I decided to walk through the wood which ran parallel to the road.

Crossing the road I headed for the cover of the wood. It was dark and eerie in there, the light of the moon being hidden by the branches of the trees and the thick foliage. Then I stepped on a dry piece of wood that snapped with a loud noise. I got such a fright that my heart nearly jumped out of my mouth. The noise sounded like a gun shot, which not only terrified me, but frightened and startled the inhabitants of the wood. Suddenly the air above was filled with the noise of crowing, and flapping wings. There must have been hundreds of crows nesting in the branches above. The noise was quite deafening. I must get to the other side of the wood as fast as possible and let the crows settle back to rest in their nests, was my thinking, as I fled through the wood stumbling and falling over unseen broken off branches. The journey through the wood seemed endless and the darkness so thick in places that even the trees could not be distinguished.

The whole situation seemed so unreal, eerie and unnecessary. What was I doing? I should be snuggled up in my bed in the safety of my parents' home, instead of trudging through a darkened wood in the middle of the night. Then my mother's words rang in my ears, "We will not allow you to go to those religious meetings any more." I determined that no one, not even my parents, would separate me from the love of my Shepherd. A new determination made me quicken my steps, and I began to run again as a gleam of moonlight burst through the overhead foliage lighting the way ahead. As quickly as the burst of moonlight appeared, it disappeared, and I was thrust into pitch blackness. The noise of the unsettled crows in the branches above was revealing to the whole community that a stranger was in the wood. I was an intruder who was breaking the peace and serenity of this wooded area, and had caused great distress to the crows and their fledglings. I felt so guilty for my actions and had to get out of the wood as soon as possible. Groping my way through the thick darkness between the trees I emerged on the opposite side of the wood from the main road, and stepped into an open field where the light of the moon shone brightly. With a sigh of relief to be out of the darkness, I made my way along the edge of the field, and noticed that the crows were settling down. Soon not one sound of a cawing crow could to be heard. A frightening stillness filled the air, and I felt as if I was the only one in the whole world who was awake at this unreasonable hour of the night. Looking ahead, I could see that I was nearing the end of the wooded area, and was soon climbing through the barbed wire fence that separated the field from the road. As I emerged at the far side of the wood, I was delighted to find myself under the full light of the moon and twinkling stars above.

Turning left, I headed down the road towards Botany Bay and our little house by the sea. This was just a side road, so I did not expect any passing cars. Strangely, I have no remembrance of the next four miles walk. I have no recollection of walking past the Old Chapel and the graveyard. That part of the walk is a total blank in my mind. I have often wondered if my Shepherd picked me up and translated me to my destination. The next thing I remember is kneeling by the well, and drinking water from my cupped hand. I then made my way over to our little house, listening to the familiar sound of the waves crashing on the sea shore. I was aware of the peace and presence of my Shepherd and felt secure at home once again. Climbing in through the window at the back of the house which had no locking latch, I sat down in a corner and fell into an exhausted sleep.

My next recollection was my mother's angry voice saying, "She is in here!" Addressing me through the window she said, "Come out here. I have the mind to give you a good hiding for the trouble you have caused us." I got off lightly with only a few slaps, but her words as well as the words of my step-father were like arrows piercing my heart. "We have had enough of your religious mania. Look how unstable it has made you, running away in the middle of the night. You don't know how worried we have been, or the trouble you have caused."

I had to comply and accept the fact that they would not allow me to attend the Fellowship meeting as long as I lived under their roof. Mother started working as a cook in the canteen of a new Gas Station that had recently been built in a neighboring village. Harry, my stepfather, also got work there, which meant he lived at home. This also meant that I was in charge of my two younger sisters. At the end of each school day, I had to cook for the three of us, wash all the dishes, polish our school shoes, and keep the house clean and tidy. Every Saturday, when all my friends were out side playing, I was indoors thoroughly cleaning the three bedrooms and bathroom, which Mother inspected when she got home. Doing her regular inspection, she saw that I missed dusting the handles of the chest of drawers in my sisters' room. Mother was angry, and told me that I was careless and slovenly. She stripped the beds in all three rooms, and made me clean them all over again. Her motto was, "Cleanliness is next to godliness!" I never again forgot to dust the handles of the chest of drawers.

Mother and Harry started to go out to the local pub every Friday evening, leaving me as the baby sitter in charge of my sisters. Then it got to the point that they were not content with only Friday night drunkenness. They started going out on Saturday nights also. Then they started to invite their drinking friends home after the pub closed. They drank till the early hours of the morning, until their carry outs ran dry. Then everyone staggered out of our door. I hated what they were doing. I hated their noisy drinking parties. I hated to see them drunk. I hated getting up in the mornings and clearing away their empty beer cans and ashtrays. The house smelled like a brewery.

The years passed and life continued along the same path. One particular evening in the midst of a drinking party, Harry called my name from the bottom of the stairs, "Isabel, come down here!"

"What do you want me for?"

"Don't be so impudent, just do what I tell you!"

Slipping on my dressing gown, I obeyed with pounding heart, and found the lounge full of people, some even sitting on the floor. As I entered the room, Harry handed me a can of beer, and said, "Come on, join the fun and let us see a smile on your face for a change."

"I don't want to drink that!"

I refused to take the can of beer from his outstretched hand. His face went red with rage and he shouted, "Take it and drink it. I am fed up looking at your sour face!"

Someone else said, "It will make you happy."

Mother rose from her chair, took the beer from Harry and put it in my hand and with a slurred voice said, "For

God's sake, girl, stop being so serious about everything. Life was made for living."

I swallowed my words, not daring to say anything, as Harry's drunken beady eyes were staring at me. I drank straight from the can, and it did not taste too bad. My mother was very happy that I was no longer 'looking down my nose at them' as she put it, and handed me a second beer.

It became a regular habit for me to join them downstairs when they came home from the pub every Friday and Saturday night. My younger sisters were not going to be left out. They also came downstairs and sipped on their parent's beer. The attitude of both Harry and my mother changed towards me. They became kinder and more considerate, which made life a little happier. By the time I was fifteen years old, I could drink them all under the table, and had started smoking. Instead of rising to the mess in the morning, I got into the routine of clearing up when everyone left, before going to bed. I made the best of my deal, and decided that I would leave home as soon as I was old enough. At the age of sixteen, I applied for a position as nanny to a family near Edinburgh and was accepted, so I left Crimond to start a new life.

Chapter Four

With the passing of the years I sensed there was something missing in my life and I could not discover what it was. I became restless and dissatisfied and decided that I needed to find my true father, and set about the task of finding out where he lived. After investigations, I found his address and decided to present myself to him. With my hand on the gate, ready to walk down the driveway and knock on his door, the voice of my Shepherd, which had been silent for many years, spoke within me. "Turn around and walk away." I could not disobey that voice, and immediately did an about turn and walked away. The desire to know my earthly father was removed from me. What ever was behind that gate did not have God's approval, so that was the end of that little episode.

I moved to Norwich in England, and took up employment with a well-known insurance company, thinking that this new challenge would satisfy my restless heart. I could not find the way back to the Shepherd I had known, loved and adored as a child. Yet I knew without a shadow of doubt that it was His voice that had spoken the words, "Turn around and walk away." I remembered the words of the shepherd who cared for sheep in the fields at Botany Bay. He had said, "A shepherd knows his own sheep. If a sheep gets lost it sits down and waits for the shepherd to find it." I was like a lost sheep, and felt forlorn, restless and dissatisfied. All I could do was wait for my Shepherd to find me. A knowing began to grow in my heart that He was drawing me back into a relationship with Him. Walking with my Shepherd would be the only thing that would satisfy my restless heart and give me peace. Then one day during the course of my business one of my clients gave me a poem. The verse of the poem that stood out and spoke to me was "Each blade of grass is given its own drop of dew daily." Through the little poem, God revealed to me that He had never left nor forsaken me. Although I had not been aware of the fact, my Shepherd had been watching over me and providing for me. The following week the same customer asked me to accompany her to a Christian meeting. As I walked into the meeting, the peace of God that I had known as a child flooded my being, and I realized that I had lived my life apart from God since the age of ten.

I then entered back into a personal relationship with my Shepherd, bought a Bible and started to read His word, and commune with Him in prayer. The overwhelming desire of my heart was to know and love my Shepherd as I had done as a child. It was then that the Lord led me to a Pentecostal Fellowship, where I was baptized the Bible way by full immersion.

It was late October in the year 1979 and I was driving to work. It was a beautiful morning. The sun was shining in a cloudless blue sky, the world around me seemed aflame with the glow of gold and russet autumn colours. My heart was running over with joy and happiness. I was back in the fold under the loving protection, guidance and peace of my Redeeming Shepherd. My heart's desire was to praise and worship Him. For a moment I lifted my hands from the steering wheel, threw them in the air, and cried out, "Jesus, I love you, and give myself to you one hundred percent. All that I am, and all that I have, take me, and use me for your glory."

The following Sunday the preacher preached on the subject, "You shall receive power after the Holy Ghost has come upon you." Initially, sinners are granted repentance by the amazing mercy and drawing power of God's grace, through hearing, believing and responding to the gospel of the crucified, resurrected Lord Jesus. As we respond to God's grace through believing the testimony of our resurrected Lord Jesus, and accept Jesus as our sin bearer and Saviour the Holy Ghost comes and takes up residence within us, and performs the miracle of regeneration. Our spirit that was dead in trespass and sin is joined to the indwelling Holy Ghost, and creates a brand new creature in the image and likeness of Jesus – perfectly holy and righteous. Our regenerate spirit cannot sin because it is born of God, but our unregenerate flesh continues to have a drive to sin, and will not know sinless perfection until we are clothed in immortality. First God comes to live in us, and then He comes upon us, to endue us with power to be His witnesses. The evidence that God has come upon a believer and endued them with power is the same as was experienced on the day of Pentecost. They spoke in other languages, by the miraculous power of the Holy Ghost.

At the end of His preaching, the preacher asked if anyone desired to be endued with Holy Ghost power, for the glory of Jesus. It was as if a huge magnet got hold of me and drew me to the altar. Kneeling, I raised my hands in the air in total submission and prayed, "Jesus my Shepherd, please endue me with power for your glory."

It was like a dam bursting. Words in a different language poured out of me like a flood. I do not know how long I knelt there, I was oblivious to what was going on around me, my spirit was communicating directly with God. It did strike me that everyone in the church must be hearing the flood of words that were pouring out from God's Spirit within. It was a supernatural miraculous experience, which left me in no doubt that I was endued with the power of the Holy Ghost. In his time the Lord would teach me how to

31

release that power that the world may know that Jesus is the same yesterday, today and forever.

I had been reading the gospel of Mark, and turned to read the final chapter before retiring for the night. The great commission hit me like a fireball exploding within my heart. I knew this was the ministry that lay ahead of me, preaching the gospel, casting out demons, speaking in tongues, and laying my hands on the sick. I was confident that God was working with me, confirming His own word with signs following, just as He did with the apostles. It had already started to happen. The Lord had led me through the first stages. I was born again as a child, now I was endued with Holy Ghost power, and could speak in tongues, in the language of the Holy Ghost. Closing my Bible, I knelt by my bed with arms raised in submission, and prayed in Holy Ghost tongues for the second time that evening. It was a gift from God, through which Jesus would be glorified in my life, but when and how remained to be seen.

The preacher the following Sunday was a man named David Ellis, who had been on a mission to the Philippines. He made an altar call at the end for anyone who felt "called of God." That enormous magnet was there again. I could not resist its drawing power, and I was once again kneeling at the altar with arms raised in total submission. "Lord, take me and use me for your glory." I stood and turned round and said, "I am going to the Philippines to preach the gospel, cast out devils, speak in tongues, lay my hands on the sick, and God will work with me confirming His word with signs following." I do not think anyone in the congregation believed me. They looked upon me as a carnal Christian, who was not complying with their church code of holiness, because I still smoked.

My prayer that evening was, "Lord, how can I go the Philippines. What about my home and work?" The voice of my Shepherd spoke within me and said, "Sell what you own and give up your work." I never questioned the voice of my Shepherd. His words were spoken with loving gentleness. At the same time they carried a note of firmness and authority, which commanded obedience. After the mid-week bible study, I approached the Pastor and told him that God had spoken to me and told me to sell what I owned, give up my work and go to the Philippines. He was kind but firm, and said, "You can't just take off and go on the mission field with no experience or Bible training. You must spend at least six months in Bible College. The Lord has no place for a novice on the mission field. I am sorry but I have to tell you that you can't go." My response to the Pastor was, "I will pray and get further confirmation from the Lord."

"Have you stopped smoking yet?"

"No! I am not justified or sanctified in God's sight by my abstinence and good performance, but by the death, blood and resurrection of Jesus. My robe of righteousness is Christ's imputed righteousness, which I wear as a garment by faith."

He held out his hand, and we shook hands, and he said, "I will pray for you, Isabel."

"Thank you Pastor." Turning away I headed for the door.

In the privacy of my home, I took the situation before the Lord. "Heavenly Father, I come to you in the name of Jesus my Shepherd, you are everywhere present and see and hear all things. You heard the conversation between the Pastor and me. Please speak to me by the power of your Spirit within, and give me confirmation of your will concerning me going to the Philippines."

His response, was swift and certain and without compromise. "Can you stand and fulfill my plan for your life, though people rise up in opposition against you?"

"Yes, Lord!" was my certain reply. As a child I had no option but to obey my mother and stepfather, who drew me away from my Shepherd into a worldly life style. I was no longer a child and was free to make my own decisions. The decision was made according to the leading of the Lord and no amount of well-meaning human reasoning or opposition would stop me. I had experienced all that as a child, and had learnt from it.

I took immediate action. The following day I rang the estate agents and put the sale of my home into operation. I also wrote a letter of resignation to my employer, which I presented to him that same afternoon.

"I don't quite know how to tell you this, but I might as well get it over as fast as possible. I have come to hand in my resignation."

He blinked in surprise, but said nothing, so I hurriedly ploughed on looking him straight in the eye. "God has called me to sell all I own, give up my employment, and go to the Philippines."

"God has WHAT!" he demanded, the look of absolute incredibility, and total unbelief, showing in his eyes and facial expression.

"I was not aware of the fact that you are religious. You have been influenced by the religious cranks on your agency."

His reasoning was the same as that of my mother and stepfather, however this time I was not a child and would not be dissuaded.

"I refuse to accept your resignation at this point. You need time to get over this religious harassment", he said with concern and pity.

Here we go again, I thought!

One week later I returned to hand over my letter of

resignation.

"So you have not had a change of heart?"

"No Sir!" I replied, firmly shaking my head. With the mind of an intelligent business man, he leant forward and asked in a tone of studied reasonableness, as he tried to get me to see sense, "What are you going to do when you arrive in the Philippines?"

"God will lead and guide me"

"Have you any kind of missionary training?"

"No"

"What about the language? Will you be able to communicate with the people?"

"I can only speak English."

A note of exasperation began to creep into his measured questions.

"I don't want to go on at you Miss Chapman, but the whole thing sounds just too absurd to me." If what I had already told him was so unacceptable to the reasoning of his carnal mind, I thought I might as well lay the full picture before him.

"I will preach the gospel, cast out devils, speak in tongues, lay hands on the sick and God will work with me confirming His word by performing miracles."

He was flabbergasted. He reached out his hand and accepted my letter of resignation, not wanting to hear any more. He rose to his feet, to show the interview had come to an abrupt end. As we shook hands he kindly suggested that I take a holiday and see a psychiatrist. Like my mother and Harry my boss also thought I had religious mania and needed help.

I decided to go home to Scotland to see my mother before flying abroad. She had changed her life style, after losing her husband and youngest daughter who were both alcoholics. She had decided to reform her life. Mother needed more than reformation, she needed the regeneration which cannot happen without God's word being planted in the heart. My mission to Scotland was surrounded by prayer. Fervently I prayed that my mother would be willing to allow me to read the scriptures to her, that she might be born of the Holy Ghost. She was a changed woman, and very open to the scriptures. God's grace granted her repentance (Acts11: 18) and she received Jesus as her sin bearer and Saviour, and accepted her forgiveness, by grace through faith in the promises of God's word, and was able to forgive herself also. The mission was successfully accomplished. Both Mother and I were "In Christ", the only safe place to be, and all the hurts of days gone by could no longer hurt or condemn. Praise the wonderful name of Jesus.

The contents of my home were gone. Some sold, others given away as gifts. My notice was worked, and my flight ticket was in my hand luggage. My cousin in Scotland had given me the address of a mission in the Philippines, so everything was falling into place. The sale of my bungalow was in the hands of my solicitor, and arrangements for a trustworthy friend to be given power of attorney were all in order. Kneeling in prayer I asked the Lord God to bless what had been my home, and its future occupants, and submitted my will and life into the charge of my Shepherd, who would lead and guide me by the power of His indwelling Spirit. Locking the door of my home behind me for the last time, I stepped out into the cold, damp drizzling rain of a January morning. A new door was opening.

Chapter Five

S moking or non-smoking?" asked the stewardess sweetly. Having smoked the last cigarette in the packet in the smokers' boarding lounge, I determined to reform myself of this bad habit. I had asked the Lord to remove this "thorn in my flesh" at least three times and nothing happened. So I decided that there were certain things we had to do for ourselves, by our own will and determination. "Non smoking" was my reply. Once I was seated in the non-smoking section of the plane, the engines soon began to rev up for take off, then we were moving along the runway at top speed, the nose of the plane started to rise and suddenly we were airborne. Within minutes the plane was engulfed in overcast clouds and the earth beneath disappeared from view. Higher and higher the plane rose, until it broke through the thick blanket of grey cloud. The new scene was breathtakingly beautiful, the sun was shining and the clouds were a brilliant white, dazzling white. The other passengers began to pull down their shutters, to shut out the shimmering brilliance of the scene, and I did the same when I began to see stars in front of my eyes.

I reached into my hand luggage to get my Bible, and a thought suddenly came to mind. "You are all alone in this big bad world. No one will be waiting to greet you when you arrive at your destination."

Then I remembered the Pastor's parting words, "Do not be too proud to come back and admit you were wrong."

Then another voice spoke to my mind.

"You fool, just look at what you have done. You have given up a good job, practically given all your furniture away for half its value and your home is up for sale."

My mind was being bombarded with negative thinking.

"You believe you are called of God. Your actions have been far from responsible. You have religious mania."

With that last remark the devil gave himself away as the accuser of the brethren. He had accused me of the same thing as a child through my parents, he had accused me through my boss, and he had accused me through the Pastor. Now he was speaking directly to my mind. Rising from my seat, I went to the toilet to deal with devil. I could not deal with him in my seat, in case the passenger next to me thought me weird for talking to myself.

Locked in the toilet I took authority over the devil.

"In the name of Jesus Christ of Nazareth, I bind you and tie you up in spiritual chains and render you powerless to continue this attack on my mind. Go now. It is written, obey Christ's name. I refuse to listen to your negative lies."

Returning to my seat I prayed silently saying, "Lord, please talk to me from your word." Opening the Bible at random my eyes fixed on Proverbs chapter three verse five.

Trust in the Lord with all thine heart, and lean not unto your own understanding.

In all thy ways acknowledge him, and he shall direct thy paths.

God's word always imparts peace to a troubled soul. His peace that passes all understanding flooded my being, and I rested in the Lord's promise that He would indeed direct my paths, as I acknowledged Him in all my comings and goings.

Leaning back in my seat I simply enjoyed God's peace, which calmed and comforted my heart and I drifted into a peaceful sleep as the noise of the engines droned on. Many hours later I was woken by the sound of an announcement over the intercom. The hostess was advising the passengers to fasten their seat belts in preparation for landing in Bangkok in approximately fifteen minutes. Passengers would be allowed to disembark for one hour and thirty minutes while the plane was refueling.

Stepping out onto the gangway, I was hit by a wall of heat and dazzling sunlight such as I had never before experienced. The woollen suit I was wearing perfectly fitted the damp, cold, drizzle of an English January, but had a smothering effect in the tropical heat of Bangkok. Within a very short period of time the suit was wet with perspiration, changing into something lighter was a must. I bought a simple brightly colored cool cotton dress at the airport terminal and immediately changed clothes.

Would it be as hot as this in the Philippines I wondered? I had never experienced such heat and humidity. Feeling more comfortable in my tropical attire, I began to look around the airport and observed that the majority were dark-skinned people. Of course I could not understand the language, but it was a friendly atmosphere and I enjoyed the bright colours worn by the locals.

Suddenly temptation stood before me in the form of a cigarette peddler. People were buying one cigarette, lighting it from a lighter that was attached to the stall by a string, and walked off happily puffing away. My determination and resolve broke, and I bought one and lit up. By the time I had smoked half of that cigarette I was stricken by guilt and condemnation, and felt as if I was displeasing the Lord, and determined never to smoke again. But I did! The plane was refueled, and the passengers were seated ready for take off. Next stop was Manila, the capital of the Philippines. We were due to arrive mid afternoon local time.

The heat and humidity was much the same as in Bangkok, quite unbearable for one born and bred by the North Sea in Scotland, with its cold biting north winds.

First I had to pass through Immigration then Customs. The Customs official was more approachable than the Immigration officer, so I asked if it would be easy to find a hotel. His English was very good and he gave instructions in his local dialect to a lady official with a friendly smile, who took me to the taxi rank.

The traffic in Manila was nose to tail, with black fumes spewing out of exhaust pipes, making me feel quite sick. I covered my nose with my hanky to avoid breathing in the smelly fumes. I was so glad to get off the traffic-jammed main streets, and the taxi driver found a very nice hotel. The bellboy soon had my luggage in the lift and we were headed for the room allocated to me. It was a comfortable clean room with air conditioning. All I wanted to do was sleep. Snuggling down between cool crisp white sheets, I whispered, "Thank you, Lord, for a safe journey. Good night."

I woke next morning with a sense of joy and expectancy. Slipping to my knees I committed the day into the Lord hands, and asked for his guidance and protection throughout. I spent the next hour praying in tongues. Paul prayed in tongues more than them all, and was mightily used by God. I decided to follow his example, that I might also be mightily used by God. Having built myself up in the Spirit, I needed to feed my flesh, and realized that I was very hungry. Lunch on the plane the previous day had been my last meal. The breakfast buffet was beautifully and artistically laid out with various fruits that I had never seen before. There were also several kinds of meats, fish and cheeses. All that I ate can be summed up in one word, delicious! I packed up my hand luggage and was ready for the final stage of the journey. The bellboy hailed a taxi to drive me to the bus station.

The bus journey turned out to be an eight hour bus

ride. The mission in San Fernando was a place to rest and get acquainted with the heat and humidity, and general life in the Philippines, before moving on further north to more remote areas. Pastor Abbey was planning a two week mission to some of the remote areas he had visited in the past. The purpose of the visit was to encourage the Pastors and brethren, and let them know that although they lived in remote mountain villages they were part of Christ's body, loved, prayed for and not forgotten.

The date was set and the day arrived. When all was ready we piled into what the brethren called a jeepney, which is a small truck, lined with seats on either side. This particular vehicle was well worn and well travelled. The seats had lost their padding, so I did not envisage a comfortable journey, God's grace would be sufficient. The sides of the vehicle were open, lending no protection from heat or dusty mountain tracks. The first two hours of the journey went tolerably well, as the roads were built of concrete, and the open sides afforded a nice cool breeze as the truck sped on its way. The bone shaking seat was the biggest problem. So we all sang praises to the Lord, which took our minds off the fact that if it were not for God's grace and enabling power we would all have back injuries by the time we reached our destination.

The driver suddenly applied the brakes forcibly, which caused all eyes to look ahead. The concrete road had simply come to an abrupt end. Our driver continued on along a narrow dirt track which started to climb up the mountain. The truck was labouring in second gear most of the time, and the track became more stony and bumpy with every kilometer. The heat of the mid day sun beat down upon us, causing all of us to wipe the perspiration from our faces every few minutes.

I was seated near the back of the truck and as I looked

behind, I was amazed at what we had been able to pass. Up and up we climbed, and being a driver myself I could tell by the sound of the engine which gear the driver was using. When he had to double de-clutch into first gear I prayed in the power of the Holy Ghost, which blotted out thoughts of the jeepney hurtling backwards and disappearing over the edge. Dust was now a big problem. The vehicle and its passengers were moving in a constant cloud of dust thrown up from the wheels. We had to tie handkerchiefs over our noses and mouths to avoid breathing in the dust, and I noticed that the dust was affecting everyone's eyes. We were all squinting through streaming half-closed eyelids. My companions had left the mission with shiny jet-black hair and brown faces. Now their hair was literally grey, and their faces covered with a film of grey dust.

It was a long painful journey. Hour after hour we crawled at snail speed up the mountainside enshrouded by dust. The singing stopped and every one was quietly having a time of meditation in their hearts with the Lord. The dirt track was becoming dangerously narrow and the wheels of the jeepney were literally only inches from the edge of the cliff, which dropped sheer down the valley thousands of feet below us. One false move by the driver would have us all hurtling down the mountainside into the river which snaked its way along the valley so far beneath us. It would definitely be a quick exit home to glory. I prayed quietly, "Dear Father in Heaven, thank you that our guardian angels are traveling with us, watching over us and keeping us safe. Please let your power control the wheels, the steering, the brakes and our driver. Please do not allow the wheels to slip over the edge, I ask in the name of the Lord Jesus."

Looking around the jeepney at my companions, I could see that all eyes were closed. They were obviously feeling the need to pray and commune with the Lord, even as I had done. All at once the jeepney came to a standstill. Ahead, the driver spotted that part of the track had been eroded away during the past rainy season, when this particular track became a rushing river cascading its way down the mountainside at great speed. It looked as though a giant had taken a bite out of the mountainside, such was the force of floodwaters during the rainy season, which caused landslides similar to the scene we were looking at. It was impossible to turn the jeep and go back, and I, for one, did not relish the idea of being driven in reverse gear backwards down this treacherous mountainside. We were stuck, there was no turning space, and the way ahead had been eroded away.

It was an old vehicle, if the brakes failed …I stopped my negative thinking abruptly, realizing that my thinking was giving way to fear, which was opposite to faith. According to 2 Timothy 1:7 "God has not given us the spirit of fear; but of power, and of love, and of a sound mind." The spirit of fear brings torment if given its own way, so I spoke to that evil spirit of fear, and commanded it to depart from me in the name above all names, the Lord Jesus Christ. With renewed peace and confidence I joined my companions who had left the jeepney and walked on up the dirt track to examine the damage. Our driver knew this mountain track like the back of his hand. Lengthy discussions were going on between the driver and the pastor, but it fell on deaf ears as far as I was concerned as I could not understand the language. One thing I was learning about Filipino culture was that they did not 'give in or give up easily', but looked for a way whereby they could implement a remedy. All the men in our group went to work collecting big boulders from the landslide area, whilst the ladies explained the solution to me.

They were going to do a quick repair job and build up

the area that was too narrow for the jeepney to pass. There was no fear in them, and by the grace of God their hearts were set on reaching our destination. Standing in the scorching heat watching the men at work I decided to examine the situation for myself, and measured the width of the track at the narrowest point of the bite. It measured seven of my size feet. Wandering back to the jeepney, I measured its width, eight of my size feet. The dirt track was one foot too narrow, at its most treacherous point. Within an hour the remedy was completed, and it was time to get back into the jeepney and press on. "Pastor, I would like to lay hands on the vehicle and pray before we move on." He nodded his head in agreement with a great beaming smile. Everyone followed suit and all hands were laid on the jeepney as we prayed the prayer of faith and agreement. "Lord God, we know that nothing is impossible with you. If the road is not wide enough for us to pass, please carry us over the crumbled area, by your own power and might, in the name of our Lord Jesus Christ, we pray." Everyone agreed with a hearty. "Amen."

God inhabits the praises of His people, so we praised Him with all our hearts as our driver started up the engine and moved into first gear. As we moved towards the great bite, the driver pressed his foot down on the accelerator to gather speed and moved into second gear, then with the accelerator jammed flat to the board, he moved into third gear. With the high praises of God in our mouths we sped over the treacherous bite. Looking behind I saw the boulders which had been placed in the gap by the men hurtling down the mountainside. The weight of the vehicle had dislodged the repair, but the remedy, together with God's power, was sufficient to get us over the bite. Everyone clapped their hands spontaneously and burst into thanksgiving saying, "Hallelujah! Hallelujah! Praise the

Lord." By the grace and power of God, the remedy, our driver's expertise, and our God given faith, we were safely on the other side, having achieved the impossible.

The clouds of dust made it impossible to enjoy the scenery, but when the driver had to slow down to negotiate his way over rough boulders, we were able to glimpse the beauty that surrounded us. Range after range of mountains lay ahead of us and marched into the purple distance. Deep in the valley below us we occasionally caught a glimpse of the river glinting and shimmering in the sunshine. The scenic beauty was quite breathtaking. Hours ago we had passed a sign which read 7,400 feet and I wondered how much higher we had climbed since then. Hunger pangs began to grip my stomach as we had been on the road for the past six hours. I was pleased to hear the Pastor announce that we were approaching a village, where we should be able to stop and relieve ourselves, stretch our weary limbs, get a drink and something to eat.

I went with my female companions to the local public toilets, which turned out to be a single drain, with a piece of lean-to corrugated iron which afforded a little bit of privacy. The drain stank in the tropical heat, so I had my first taste of how life was lived in the primitive mountain areas. We were all covered in dust from head to foot and longed for water to be able to wash, but there was still three hours journey ahead, so it was decided that we press on in our present condition. My ears were bothering me and hearing was difficult, due to probably two things, the high altitude and the dust. My companions from the lowlands were making a great sacrifice of love in coming to the mountain Provinces. Living in the remote areas was as hard for them as it was for me, except that they were Filipino, and were more able to cope with the heat and humidity than I was.

The men sat down at the table of a local café and tucked

into rice and whatever was available, but the smell in the ladies 'comfort room' was still in our nostrils and the sight of food caused our stomachs to heave. So I and my sister companions settled for a drink of water from an enamel mug, rusted by humidity and age, which we passed from one to another. Climbing back into the jeepney, we settled down for the final phase of this particularly hazardous journey. Just another three hours and we would be able to wash the dust and grime from our bodies.

By the grace of God we arrived safely at our destination as the jeep pulled up outside a little home made of bamboo, which was perched on top of four stilts. The occupants came hurrying out to meet their brethren and we were greeted with great warmth and love. Regardless of our filthy, smelly state they were overjoyed to see us and warm embraces were shared all around. I saw the love of Jesus in action in the lives of my travelling companions, who had left their homes and families behind to face a treacherous most uncomfortable journey for the edification of their mountain brethren. Love never fails!

The lady of the house ushered me and my sister travelling companions into one small room. The only piece of furniture was a single bed made of bamboo with no mattress. My sisters knew what to expect. They had been there before, they were the channels God used to bring the knowledge of His word which had imparted new life to this precious family. Now they were waiting to see how I was going to handle the situation. "The bed has been especially made for you Sister Chapman, here in the mountain Provinces every one sleeps on the bamboo floor." I was amazed as I tried to take in this new scene. It was all a great cultural shock to me. There I stood, filthy dirty, exhausted, ravenous, thirsty, with aching bones, having experienced the most horrendous journey of my life, to find I had to sleep on a hard bamboo bed.

Suddenly my sisters started grinning from ear to ear, obviously trying hard not to laugh. My facial expression of shock and incredulity combined with my dirt streaked face had touched their funny spot, and they were doing all in their power to try and stop laughing, which might have offended me. The situation was indeed so incredibly awful that one could only laugh or cry. Now they had my attention, because I could not see what they were finding so funny. Looking at their expression of expectancy, their grey hair, their dirty streaked faces, and the fact that they had set out on this journey willingly, as a mission of love, released God's grace into the situation and I began to laugh. One by one they came and hugged me, and we all laughed and laughed and laughed until we were doubled over with stitches in our sides. Tears of joy streamed down our faces and mingled with the dust, which made us look as if we were painted up for some tribal war dance. Eventually we pulled ourselves together, and I knew that God's amazing grace, and the enabling power of the indwelling Holy Ghost, would allow me to cope with whatever situation He led me into.

I needed God's amazing grace and enabling power much sooner than I expected. There was no shower or bathtub at the house. During the past nine hour journey the dirt and grime had worked its way into every pore in my body, and made my hair feel like straw. My next discovery was that there was no water on tap. The water came from an underground well and had to be pumped up by hand. Worst of all the pump was situated in the middle of the yard in full view of everyone. As I went to investigate the pump, a little girl ran ahead of me and grabbed the pump handle and began to pump with vigor, as if willing the water to appear. Suddenly it splashed out of the nozzle.

Cupping my hands together to catch the water I sloshed my face a few times with cool clear water, it felt so good! Rinsing out my handkerchief I began to wipe off the dust and grime that coated my travel bag.

All the baggage was tied to the roof of the jeepney, to give the maximum legroom for the passengers. The result was that everything was impregnated with dust. Every individual garment had to be thoroughly shaken, as well as the travel bag, before I could repack my few belongings. Whilst busy on this particular chore, with the help of my beautiful, brown-eyed companion, (who had shown me how to use the pump,) my attention was diverted by the sound of metal hitting metal in sharp blows. Looking in the direction of the noise, I could see men at work rigging up corrugated tin walls around the pump. "Thank you Lord, at least I will be able to wash in privacy." Once again I saw how the Filipinos were always ready to make a remedy with whatever was at hand. One by one my grey haired companions disappeared behind the corrugated walls, and appeared once again with shiny black hair and glowing brown faces. All traces of dirt and grime had been washed away. It reminded me of the scripture, "Being washed by the water of the word." God's word acts like water, and washes away the filth and grime of sin in our lives.

It was nearly dark when I entered the newly erected washroom. My little companion was right on my heels and before I knew what was happening, she grabbed the pump handle and started pumping with the same enthusiasm and vigor as before. The nozzle was so low that I had to get on my knees to position my head under the flow of water. After three applications of shampoo, and one application of conditioner my head and neck were clean. My little companion was in control. She then fetched a big zinc basin and pumping with all her might filled it to the brim. She then said, "Tabu" and handed me a brightly coloured plastic bowl with a handle. What did she expect me to do with this? I wondered. She wrinkled her eyebrows and shook her head as if to say, "Do you not even know how to take a bath?"

She said again "Tabu". Stretching out her hand she took the tabu from me and proceeded to give me a demonstration. Dipping the "tabu" in the basin she filled it with water and poured it over the top of her head. To be sure that I got the message, she gave me a second demonstration, then handed me the tabu with a big smile and left me to get on with having my bath. It worked very well, and I left the washroom clean and shiny and very white compared to my companions. "In Christ there is neither Jew nor Greek, Filipino nor British, poor nor rich, brown nor white, male nor female: for ye are all one in Christ Jesus. (Gal 3:28)

Sunset here in the Philippines is a wondrous, glorious sight. The heavens are aglow with God's glory. The sky changes from tropical blue with white puffy clouds to differing shades of reds with dark purple clouds. It is the time of day when the heavens declare the glory of Almighty God, the Great Creator of all things. As the sun begins to set it appears like a great ball of fire in the sky, and takes approximately ten seconds to disappear from view. Then night falls like a dark curtain being drawn across the sky, every evening around 6.30 pm. Then the moon appears with multitudes of stars giving a little light to the inhabitants below.

Kerosene lamps were the only means of lighting indoors, and reminded me of the paraffin lamp we used in our little house at Botany Bay. I was so hungry I could have eaten anything. Laid out on the table before us were bowls of boiled rice and vegetables and meat in brown gravy. I prayed over the meal according to 1 Tim 4:4-5 "For every creature of God is good, and nothing to be refused, if it be received with thanksgiving. For it is sanctified by the word of God and prayer." I also prayed over the water according to Mark 16:18: "If they drink any deadly thing, it shall not hurt them." I tucked into the meal, which I thoroughly enjoyed. I had adopted the local way of eating without cutlery, pressing the food between the three fore-fingers and thumb and scooping it into my mouth. We were all exhausted and ready for sleep. We were clean, fed and watered and with a prayer of thanksgiving to the Lord for the victories of the day, the little house rocked with the sound of snoring, as the occupants fell into a happy contented deep sleep.

We remained there for two nights, and the Pastor held bible study meetings to encourage the believers to stand firm in the faith, and not to be drawn back into tradition, superstition, idolatry or witchcraft, which abounded in that area. I was sad to say good bye to my little companion who taught me how to take a bath Filipino style. When I picked her up in my arms to give her a goodbye hug, she looked into my eyes, furrowed her eye brows, shook her head, as if to say, "Don't you even know how to give a proper kiss?" and kissed me full on the lips. As I set her feet back on the ground and watched her run back to the protection of her parents, who had been our hosts, I knew that that little sheep was under divine protection. The jeepney was packed with the luggage piled on top, and once again it was warm embraces as we said goodbye and set out for our new destination higher into the unknown.

God was moving by His grace, drawing the people of the mountain Provinces to Himself, and He needed preachers who were born of His Spirit to work with Him.

Romans 10:13 -15

For whosoever shall call upon the name of the Lord shall be saved. How then shall they call on him who they have not believed? And how shall they believe in him of whom they have not heard? And how shall they hear without a preacher?

And how shall they preach, except they are sent?

It was time for my travelling companions to return to San Fernando to their families and ministries there, but I was led to remain in the mountains. We had arrived in Tabuk, Kalingao Apayao and were residing in the home of Pastor and Mrs. Teckney. We arrived weary, dirty, hungry and thirsty and were received with the normal warm loving Filipino welcome. Pastor Teckney's home was a little more up-market compared to the homes I had lived in over the past two weeks. I had a room with a bed, which was dressed with a very comfortable mattress, pillows, sheets and a blanket, necessary to keep one warm overnight. The temperature was much cooler in the higher altitudes of Kalingao Apayao. After sleeping on hard bamboo beds or floors for the past two weeks, the comfortable mattress was sheer luxury.

As the only remaining guest in the Teckney household, I was able to spend time in fellowship with this godly man. He told me that he and his co-workers had regularly and sincerely prayed for the salvation of the headhunting tribes people in the remote northern mountains of Kalingao Apayao. Also that God would send a preacher from another country. He reasoned that the tribes people would be more inclined to listen to a foreigner than a native Filipino.

Chapter Six

"**W**hy are you here in this remote mountain Province?" asked Pastor Teckney. Opening my Bible I turned to Mark chapter sixteen and read the Great Commission.

"I am here to preach the gospel, pray in tongues, cast out devils, lay my hands on the sick and God will work with me confirming His word with signs following."

"Have you done this before Sister Chapman?"

"I have started by coming here. Jesus said, 'Go into all the world.' I speak in tongues, but I have not yet had the opportunity to obey the other instructions."

"I will accept that you are the answer to our prayers. A white woman on her own in this dangerous remote region is unheard of. I must give you the opportunity to fulfill our Lord's commission. Tomorrow, I will begin to make arrangements for a mission to the headhunting tribal areas in the mountain regions."

During the evening meal and afterwards, Pastor Teckney described how he had visited certain areas where they still practiced headhunting as a tradition. At that time there was particular unrest among the tribes. On one occasion villagers rose after the midday siesta to face a tribal war party heading in their direction, and they were not a welcoming sight being slashed with war paint and armed with spears and knives. The villagers, especially the women and children, were terrified and overwhelmed with grief at the thought of losing their husbands and fathers. The men of the community refused to run and give up their land and property, and would fight only in self-defence. Pastor

Teckney had taken control of the situation under the leading of the Holy Ghost and instructed every one to go to their native bamboo built Fellowship building and pray. The little wooden structure was packed with believers and non believers. Everyone, even the non believers and the children, began to cry out to God to move on their behalf and save them from being attacked by the fierce murderous approaching war party.

Darkness fell and they lit a kerosene lamp. As they waited Pastor Teckney preached to the unbelievers and they all accepted Christ as the only true Saviour of sinners. He comforted every one with the scriptures concerning death being the door into heaven, never to die again. Hours passed, and the expected attack had not come, and the praise leaders started praising the Lord. One by one all the people began to praise God, who inhabits the praises of His people. Unknown to the believers God was working on their behalf.

It was decided by the majority that the headhunters would not attack at that late hour in the darkness of night, but with the rising of the sun first thing in the morning. It was unanimously agreed that all should return to their own houses to rest and pray and be ready for the expected attack with the first light of morning.

A new day dawned with the inhabitants of that particular mountain village once again gathered in the bamboo Church building. As the God of the universe rolled back the darkness of night and touched that area with the light of morning, the inhabitants were praising God that they were alive, and that all was well with them. They sang and praised and waited expectantly for the first sounds of the warrior war cries. Time passed and nothing happened. Eventually the men ventured outside to investigate and found no signs of an approaching war party They decided to send out a search party in case the warriors were still lurking in the vicinity. The search party returned with two young warriors who were hiding in the branches of a tree. They were unable to explain why they had not left with the war party, but said they were constrained by a powerful force to remain. They testified that their Chief had decided to launch the attack with the setting of the sun the previous evening. As they headed in the direction of the village they saw hundreds of lighted torches burning all around the village. The nearer they got the brighter the lights became, and they decided to retreat, believing that they were heavily outnumbered. There was a spontaneous round of applause and thanksgiving to the Lord, for all knew that the previous evening everyone had been indoors on their knees in prayer as the sun set and darkness fell. God had sent his holy angels to take up their positions all around the village. In the eyes of the enemy they had appeared as bright shining lights.

The angels of the lord encampeth round about them that fear him, and delivereth them. Psalm 34:7

It was the amazing grace of God that compelled the two young warriors to remain when the rest of their company retreated in fear. They were astounded by the fact that the villagers were on their knees in prayer when the attack was scheduled to take place. They were even more amazed to hear that the burning torches were the brilliance of God's holy angels. They wanted to know this God who had sent His angels to protect His people. They removed their war paint and settled down in the village, and with the passing of time their minds were renewed by knowledge of God's word and they were indwelt by the Holy Ghost. The two brothers were often heard crying out to God in prayer for the salvation of their Chief and family whom they had deserted. The same power that compelled them to remain in the village also compelled them to go back to their own tribe to share the good news of the Gospel of their Lord Jesus Christ.

Pastor Teckney went on to explain that the mountains of Northern Luzon were no place for a European woman unless she was sent by God. There are head hunters, rebel groups such as the NPA – New Peoples Army, hiding out in the mountains. "You have to face the fact that that we could all be murdered up there."

"Pastor, we are not going up there to be murdered by headhunters or the NPA, we are going there to prove to these people that the One True Living God loves them, and has made a way of escape from eternal damnation for them."

"It thrills and excites my spirit to hear you talk like this. Does this mean that God is leading you to go ahead?"

"I did not come here according to my plan, but according to God's will, plan and purpose. We must go!"

The matter was settled. Pastor Teckney replied, "We will leave in three days time. In the mean time we will pray and fast, if so led, and seek the face of God."

We would be a company of only six people as some backed out at the last minute. Our guide, was a government employee who worked in the mountain regions on a part time basis, and knew the majority of the tribal dialects. Our baggage carriers, were two young men who were hungry for a deeper walk with God. The rest of the group was Pastor Teckney, his daughter Susan and me. On the appointed day at dawn we ventured out into the unknown. The Pastor had hired a jeepney with a driver to take us as far as possible by road, and when it petered out a pony and cart carried us along a dirt track until we came to the banks of a river. The rest of the journey would be on foot. The bare necessities of our baggage were unloaded, including

Susan's guitar, which she decided to carry herself. Heading towards the river our guide stepped into the water with his luggage balanced on top of his head. Our baggage bearers followed suit. I stepped into the water fourth in line, followed by Susan, and her father took up the rear position. The water was brown and muddy to begin with, but when we reached the half way point the water became crystal clear. We were in water up to our waists and had to push against a strong undercurrent to remain on our feet. I noticed Pedro our guide turning round to satisfy himself that I was still on my feet and had the strength to withstand the force of the undercurrent. I did have a few shaky moments when I had to struggle to keep my balance. At such times I prayed in the Holy Ghost for He is our enabler. It was easy after we had passed the halfway mark. The water level dropped and the undercurrent was hardly felt. Within an hour we were all safely on the other side and sat down for ten minutes rest.

The river bordered onto flooded rice paddies which were separated by small mud dykes. Each dyke was approximately a foot wide. It felt like walking on a tightrope and I kept slipping off the dyke into the muddy rice field, so decided to walk in the water along the edge of the dyke. I kept losing my shoes which got stuck in the mud, and I realized that I was falling too far behind our leader and slowing up the rest of the party behind me. There was only thing to do, carry my shoes and go barefoot, but I was aware that there were blood-sucking leeches in the water and I did not relish the thought of having leeches fixed onto my feet and ankles. Plucking my shoes out of the mud and setting off at a faster pace barefoot, I spoke to the Lord. "This is a matter of faith, Lord; I trust that you will not allow one of these leeches to fasten itself onto my flesh. In the name of your Son Jesus I pray". Faith moves God to move on our behalf, and I never experienced being zapped by a leech.

We left the rice paddies behind and continued up the mountain slopes. On and on we hiked with the perspiration running down our bodies in rivulets. My clothes were ringing wet. The unrelenting tropical sun was glaring down at us, burning into my skin. I was beginning to struggle. How much longer would I be able to keep up the pace under these conditions? In desperation I cried out, "Lord, please cover the sun with a black cloud. I cannot take this heat any longer." My companions said, "Amen!"

Susan was also struggling, as were the bearers carrying the baggage. The only two who appeared not to be in the slightest bit of discomfort were Pastor Teckney and Pedro our guide. They had done this journey many times in the past. We continued on and I for one was praying in tongues, drawing strength from God within. The muscles in my legs ceased to ache and strength began to replace weakness. Suddenly Pedro pointed to the sky. "Look, it is a miracle. God has answered Sister Chapman's prayer. The sun is blocked out with a dark cloud." Everyone looked up, a thing we could not have done a few minutes earlier. You cannot look directly into the brilliance of a tropical sun without damaging your eyes. "Surely this is a sign from the Almighty that we are going to see great and mighty things," said Pastor Teckney. We were all filled with the awesomeness of the presence of God, who had answered a simple cry for help by covering the sun with a cloud, and the Pastor's words filled us with great expectation.

Four hours had passed since we left the river and we were approaching the ancient world of the headhunters. Their dwelling places were little houses made of bamboo with straw roofs which provided shelter from the heat and sun as well as from the heavy rains of the rainy season. It looked like a Stone Age community, and I discovered later that the majority of their tools were made from stone. As we approached the village our guide and the Pastor started smiling and waving and turned to us and told us to do the same, which would indicate that we were friendly and did not mean them any harm. People and children emerged their houses. I was amazed to see that the children were all naked. The women were bare breasted and the men wore only a loincloth. A kindly man approached us with an earthenware vessel full of water as a gesture of good will, and we all took our turn and drank with thanksgiving and solemnity.

As we walked into the heart of the village the children ran around me shouting excitedly, "Puraw! Puraw! Puraw!"

"What does Puraw mean?" I asked my companions. "White. They have never seen a white skinned person before." The crowd grew as everyone came to see the Puraw and I became the center of attraction, but they also had my attention. Many of the men were tattooed and some had open sores running with pus. The children could not stop scratching their heads which were crawling with lice, and yellow matter was stuck around their eyes and beautiful long eye lashes. The bodies of these children had not seen water for many days. Some of women's looks were spoilt with unsightly growths under their chins. The worst ones protruded out beyond the chin. Later I discovered that the ugly growths were goiters. They were not a pretty sight. The lice, the oozing pus, the eyes stuck up with yellow matter, the goiters, and their unclean state quite repulsed me.

"Lord, how can I love these people?" I turned away and found myself standing by the water pump trying to sort out my churning emotions. The Spirit of the Lord moved in me, and I saw the people as dry bones, very dry bones without life, dead bones. They were living people but dead to God. The Spirit of the Lord said, "Prophesy to these bones and say to them: Dry bones, hear the word of the Lord, and I will make breath enter you and you will come to life. Then you will know that I am the Lord."

I became aware that I was still standing by the water pump, and had been crying out in the Spirit, in tongues, with tears rolling down my cheeks, but I had the assurance that God would put His Spirit in them and they would receive eternal life. God looks upon the heart. Man looks upon the outward appearance. Now I saw these people from God's perspective, dead lifeless bones without hope, headed towards eternal damnation. My heart was moved by the compassion and the love of Jesus for these dry bones. How much did Jesus love them? Enough to die for them! His death and blood had paid the full ransom price for all their sins. I no longer saw the condition of their flesh. I was no longer concerned about the lice or oozing pus, yellow mattered eyes and ugly goiters. They were precious lost souls and the Chief Shepherd wanted them in His fold. He would put His Spirit in them and they would receive the free gift of eternal life.

I had turned my back and walked away, not wanting to look at them. Now I turned to face them with Jesus' love for them flowing out from His Spirit within me. Stooping down I picked up a little girl, and kissed her on the cheek and wiped the matter from her eyes with my handkerchief. Then I was moving around the women giving them a warm embrace, and shaking hands with the men. The children were flocking around me, touching my white skin, even pinching me to see if I was real. Love never fails! As I moved amongst the people I saw how they were responding to love, and saw also that they had warm tender hearts that had been prepared for this time by the prayers of the saints and God's amazing grace.

One family vacated their humble home for Susan and me and moved in with a neighbour. The men in our group were welcome to share the homes of various families, our baggage was brought to us but there was no wardrobe, chest of drawers, not even a table or bed in our humble lodging house. The floor was to be our table as well as our bed. However, we were thankful, as it provided shelter from the merciless sun, and we lay down on the floor and relaxed our bodies after the long hot hike. Soon afterwards we were called to join the rest of our group for a meal which consisted of boiled rice and coffee. In spite of the fact that the rice was absolutely tasteless and the coffee too strong, I gave thanks and gratefully ate what was set down before us. The meal took away the hunger pangs which had been gnawing at my stomach for hours past.

With our hunger satisfied, Susan and I headed for the water pump where I had been standing when the Spirit of the Lord dealt with my wrong attitude of judging the people by their outward appearance. We were so disappointed to find out that the pump was out of order, and had not been used for years. Close inspection showed that it was a heap of rust, not even fit for a junkyard. We were shocked to discover that the nearest water was to be found in a mountain stream approximately an hour walk away. I was dirty and smelly after our arduous journey, but could not face another two hour trek to have a wash. This was why the villagers were so unclean – a lack of water. How terrible it must be to live constantly in such conditions. We went back to our lodging place giving up all hope of even washing our faces, but were wonderfully surprised when a young lady brought us a small bowl of water, into which we dipped our hankies and were able to wash the dust and grime from our faces and hands.

The heavens above us changed colour to a fiery red, and

the sun looked a massive ball of flame. The heavens were once again declaring the glory and power of our God. Down, down, down, the sun dropped until it disappeared from view, and the night curtain of darkness was slowly drawn over the Stone Age community. The night air became alive with strange calls and eerie sounds, especially the buzzing sound of mosquitoes hungry for their next meal of blood. Susan spoke into my thoughts as I swiped the air to drive off a mosquito that was dive-bombing me.

" So many people and children here have skin diseases because mosquito bites become infected, and flies carry the infection from one person to another. It is time we went indoors before we get bitten."

The moon was almost full and lighted the pathway to our lodgings. Susan stepped in behind me and covered the doorway with a piece of lean-to bamboo. There was no lock to the piece of lean-to bamboo that served as a door, and anyone could remove it. Taking up my position on the floor I realized that we had no windows. There were gaps in the wall through which anyone could enter the room. Thanking God in prayer that we were under divine protection, Susan and I settled down to sleep.

A few hours later I was woken by aching bones. The bamboo floor provided no comfort whatsoever. Sitting upright to move my position and rub my aching bones, I saw that my companion was sound asleep. I also noticed bright shafts of moonlight were streaming in through a gap in the wall that formed the window. Lizards darted about, feeding on the many crawling insects which came out of the straw roofing. Lying down again on my other side I could hear the sound of dogs barking, and the insidious beat of tribal drums in the distance. I remembered the testimony Pastor Teckney had shared with me about the warring tribes. In my imagination I saw a figure with a war painted face carrying a knife in his hand. A cold sweat pricked my skin. Fear and panic gripped my soul and I wanted to rise up and run. But where would I run to for safety? I was on top of a mountain in the head hunting vicinity of Northern Luzon. I covered my head with my bath towel to shut out the thoughts of a stealthy war painted figure climbing noiselessly in through the window with a long knife to claim the supreme trophy – a white head.

The spirit of fear had me in its grip and I began to pray quietly in tongues, which released the Holy Ghost into the situation, and I found myself commanding the tormenting spirit of fear to depart from me in the name of the Lord Jesus Christ. I then asked the Lord to send four angels to guard us, two to stand by our feet and two to stand by our heads. I believed they had taken up their positions as I had asked, and God's peace flooded my being and all fear was gone. "Please, Lord, let me sleep in spite of this hard floor" was my final prayer.

Morning light burst through the window and the quiet stillness of the night was replaced with the chattering of villagers going about their daily routine. "Thank you, Lord, for giving me a good night's rest in spite of the hard floor. I submit this day of my life into your hands, and trust that you will lead and guide me according to your will and plan, in Jesus' name I pray." I could hear the sound of a guitar playing and realized that Susan was already up and going about our Father's business. As I slid the lean-to door to one side I found the little basin of water sitting by the door. I washed, changed my clothes, brushed my hair and was ready to face a new day. Susan was sitting under the shade of a coconut tree surrounded by children. As I approached them I held out my arms and one by one they came and gave me a hug. Susan was teaching them a chorus in their local dialect. As I knew the words in English I taught them the actions. Soon the mothers joined in and even some of the men joined us. It was a happy hour which was thoroughly enjoyed by all, even the bystanders, because it broke the monotony of the regular routine of the day. I noticed that every girl over the age of puberty was either pregnant or had a baby at her breast. They did not have such things as push chairs, prams or cots in which to place their babies, but carried them in a sling, sometimes on their backs, sometimes across their chests to make breast feeding easy. They were all totally unselfconscious about their nakedness. They must have thought that it was extraordinary for my companions and me to be covered with clothes in tropical heat.

After a bowl of fried rice and a cup of coffee made from local grown coffee beans, the time had come for me to relieve myself. I explained my predicament to Susan, who handed me a piece of bamboo as a walking stick. Pointing to an area outside the village with thick foliage she said, "Go there and squat down. No one will see you."

"I do not need this walking stick," I said handing it back to her.

"You will need it!" she said in a very determined tone. So I set out for wooded area carrying my walking stick. At my chosen spot I squatted down and was in mid stream when I heard the movement of feet and the rustling of leaves behind me. Turning in panic I saw a black native pig approaching me. I grabbed the stick and waved it in the air, but the pig kept moving towards me. I literally had to keep the pig at a distance with the stick until I had completed my task, using a leaf for the clean up operation. Then I passed by the pig keeping it at bay with the stick. Turning round to see if it was following me I almost lost my breakfast, as the pig was relishing what I had deposited under the bush.

Susan was waiting for me at the top of the ridge. "Are you all right? Did you manage?"

We hugged and laughed. In between the laughter she apologized for not telling me.

"I just could not bring myself to tell you why you would need the stick," she said doubled over with a stitch in her side. "I had to face the same thing for the first time early this morning." This was another thing I was noticing about the character of Filipinos. When faced with a situation that was incredible and above normal acceptance, they did not moan and groan and complain, but accepted the situation and laughed, which is a much better attitude.

Walking back into the village I noticed carved statues set in places of prominence around the village.

"What is the purpose of these statues, Susan?"

"They are the people's gods. Because they do not know the One True Living God, they have made gods for themselves."

"Do you mean to say that they pray to these dumb, deaf, blind, dead statues?"

"Yes! Early this morning the entire village knelt and prayed to them for their daily needs."

Surely that had to be the theme of the meeting that was planned for that evening. I spent the rest of the day in our lodging house studying the scriptures and seeking God for the word He would have me share at the evening meeting. The Bible reveals that the gods of the heathen are idols, that an idol is nothing but a dead thing with no breath or life in it. Thus says the Lord God; "Repent, and turn yourselves from your idols" (Ezekiel 14:6). The first two commandments reveal to us God's heart concerning idols:

Thou shall have no other gods before me.

You shall not make for yourself any graven image, or any likeness of any thing in heaven... You shall not bow down thy self to them, nor serve them, for I, the Lord thy God, am a jealous God.

The sin of idolatry is a great sin in God's sight and holds people in bondage to hereditary curses. God also says that those who pray to idols, or serve idols by bowing down before them and giving offerings to them, are showing their hatred towards God Almighty, who created people for His pleasure.

(See Exodus 20:1-5 &Psalm 96:8 & Acts 15:20 & 1Cor 12:2 & 1John 5:21)

Little children keep yourselves from idols

The reason I was here in this Stone Age village was to bring the truth to these people. God wanted to bless them, but the One True God and Creator of all things cannot be approached through a blind, dumb, deaf, lifeless piece of wood or clay. The Bible teaches that there is only one way sinners can approach Almighty God. Jesus is the way, the truth, and the life.

For there is one God, and one mediator between God and men, the man Christ Jesus;

Who gave his life a ransom for all ... 1Timothy 2:5-6

Jesus died and gave his sinless life as the once and for all perfect ransom payment for the sins of the world.

Jesus rose from death, and by merit of His resurrection, broke the power of death and the grave.

Jesus ascended back into heaven to sit at the right hand of the Father, as the only mediator between sinners and our Holy God.

"Heavenly Father, I come into your presence in the name of Jesus Christ and I ask that you will anoint me as I preach your word in the meeting tonight. Convict the hearts of the hearers so that they will be willing to turn away from their idols, even destroy them, and let them see you as the only Saviour of sinners. I trust for a double anointing, which will include my interpreter. You have promised in your word to work with me, confirming your word with miraculous signs, and I trust you to do it. Amen."

Chapter Seven

All the occupants of the village, including the children,
attended the service that night held under the light of
the full moon. Pastor Teckney opened in prayer in the
dialect of the people, and then Susan led praise and
worship, playing the choruses she had already taught the
children early that morning. Everyone joined in and we had
a glorious time of praise, then the Pastor introduced me as
the preacher and to my surprise he called our guide,
brother Pedro to be my interpreter, explaining that he was
more proficient in the local dialect. Pedro had never
interpreted for a foreigner before and tried to decline, but
submitted his will to the will of God.

He was nervous even as I was nervous. I had never
actually preached the gospel before. In the flesh we were
shaking like jellies we were so unsure of ourselves. God had
brought us this far and I was convinced that the Holy Ghost
would lead us. I laid my hand on his shoulder and prayed in
the Holy Ghost. As I prayed in tongues, he burst out in
tongues, and I discovered later that this was the first time he
had prayed in the supernatural power of the Holy Ghost.
All I needed to do was make a start by faith. At that precise
moment we heard the noise of a jet in the heavens above,
probably descending for landing in Manila. Thus God set
the scene!

Pointing to the heavens above I asked if everyone could
hear the noise of the aeroplane above. Heads nodded all
around and I explained that the One true Living God who
brought the light every morning, and the dark every
evening, and the rain to water the rice in the rainy season,

told me to get on an aeroplane which would carry me to the other side of the world. Then He led me up here to your village, because He wants you to know Him. The name of the only true God is Jesus Christ. I got them to repeat the Lord's name three times, instructed by my interpreter. I explained that God came from heaven to earth and died to save sinners from damnation.

I had brought with me a small flashlight so I was able to see to read the Ten Commandments, which convinced them that they were indeed sinners who needed a Saviour. Then I asked the Chief if he would bring one of their idol gods to me, which he did. Pointing to the idol I said, "Your god has ears, but it cannot hear. It has a nose but cannot breathe, a mouth but it cannot speak. It is a dead piece of wood with no life in it. The tree is cut down; out of one part a god is carved and created. The other part of the same tree is chopped into firewood and burnt to cook rice.

Looking around at the faces waiting for a reaction, all I could see were eyes wide with amazement, as realization of this truth was hitting them. I pressed on, "This is a false god that can neither hear nor answer your prayers, it is a dead thing with neither life nor power. It is nothing but a block of carved wood. This false idol god cannot heal you if you are sick, it cannot provide your daily bread, it cannot provide you with water, but the one true God can heal the sick and provide you with water, make your crops grow, impart eternal life to your spirit, and bless you abundantly.

The one true God is all seeing, all hearing, and all knowing. He has been watching you praying to dead, dumb idols and He is jealous, because He is the one who loved you so much that He sent His son Jesus to us, and He willingly died to pay the penalty for all of your sins, and then God raised Him to life again so that His Holy Spirit can be with us always. Look around you, look at each

68

other's faces. We all have one head, two eyes, a nose and mouth, yet we are all unique individuals, no two people are identical. Who created you a unique individual? Not this false god that was been made by your own hands. God Almighty, the one who displays his Majesty and glory in the heavens above us with the setting of the sun each day, He created each and every one of us special and unique."

The Chief was still standing next to my interpreter holding the false god. Suddenly he raised his right hand summoning everyone's attention, and he began to speak. I could not understand what he was saying, but I sighed a great sigh of relief as he threw the idol to the ground. The assembled company rose in unison clapping their hands. This was their way of renouncing their false gods, and accepting Jesus as their Saviour.

"What did the Chief say?" I asked Pedro. "He said the puraw (white) preacher is right. An idol is nothing, it is not a god, and we will follow the God who created us, not a god that we have made for ourselves. We will chop up all the idols and use them as firewood to cook our rice."

The meeting was in total disarray with people coming and going as more idols were being thrown to the ground. I went to the Chief and warmly shook his hand, and asked Pedro to interpret for me as I spoke to him.

"Sir, this evening the curse has been removed from your people. From now onwards you will enjoy the blessings of the Lord God Almighty. Please ask your people to reassemble so that I can bring the meeting to a close." Immediately the Chief spoke to his people and all settled down again, and I was able to continue.

"This evening the curse has been removed from this community. From now onwards you will enjoy the blessings of Almighty God, and His Son, Jesus whom Almighty God sent to be with us and save us by dying in our place."

Having read John 3 verses 3 to 5 I continued. "Jesus said you must be 'born again'. When we are born from our mother's womb we are born of the flesh. Our body consists of three parts, body, soul and spirit. The part of us that must be born again is our spirit. Our spirit cannot die. When our mortal flesh dies our spirit is taken to one of two places, heaven to be clothed in a new immortal body to live with God forever in a new perfect world, or the lake of fire and brimstone to be eternally punished for our sins. Those who respond to God's amazing grace, believe and accept that Jesus' death and blood paid the full ransom price to cancel out our sin record. If we believe that Jesus Christ rose from the dead and ascended back to heaven, to sit at the right hand of the Father, we are granted repentance and forgiveness by the grace of God.

"If you believe and accept Jesus Christ as your sin bearer and Saviour, please stand to your feet now." Within seconds the whole community was on their feet.

"If you believe that Jesus Christ rose from death, please raise both your arms now."

All arms were raised heavenward. As the people stood before the Lord with arms raised in full submission. I prayed the following prayer,

"Lord God, thank you for your amazing grace and unconditional agape love for sinners. Thank you for granting these dry dead bones repentance. Thank you for opening their eyes to see that their idols are nothing. Thank you for drawing them to yourself by your amazing grace. Please send the Holy Ghost to breathe new life into these dry bones that they may live and receive eternal life, in the name of Jesus Christ I pray."

As I prayed in the power of the Holy Ghost I knew that the Spirit of Christ was powerfully moving in the people regenerating their spirit as the Holy Ghost took up residence within them. Tears were streaming from eyes all around as the people spoke to the Lord and received their sins forgiven by faith in the promises of God's word.

"Now let me explain what has happened within you. Your spirit that was dead in trespass and sin and cut off from the life of God, and headed towards eternal damnation, has been regenerated and joined to God by the power of the indwelling Holy Ghost, who is the Spirit of Christ. Your regenerate spirit is a brand new creation, created in righteousness and true holiness possessing the righteousness of Christ and eternal life. Even though you die, you will live again in the eternal city clothed in a new glorified immortal body. Your flesh has not been changed it will continue to have a drive for sin, but as you grow in the knowledge of God's word, your lifestyle will change. Your spirit has been born again by the indwelling Holy Ghost and cannot sin."

At that point I knew that I must obey the Great Commission in its fullness, as taught by Jesus (Mark 16:17-18). Walking over to a woman whose hands were still in the air and tears streaming down her cheeks, I laid my hand on her goiter which protruded out beyond her chin.

"In the name of Jesus Christ I address you evil spirit of infirmity, and tie you up in spiritual chains, and forever render you powerless and ineffective. Now depart from this woman. It is written! Obey the name of Jesus Christ."

Then I prayed in the Spirit in tongues, expecting God to work with me confirming His word with signs following as promised in Mark 16:20. As I prayed in tongues this released the miraculous power of God the Holy Ghost into the situation, and I felt the goiter reduce in size under my hand. My carnal mind thought "is this really happening?" In that split second of doubting the goiter grew back to its original size. The voice of my Shepherd spoke within me and said, "A double minded person is unstable in all their ways, and can receive nothing from me." Full of remorse I cried out, "Lord, forgive me!" Shutting out my carnal mind with all its unbelief, I pressed into the Spirit and laid my hand on that goiter for a second time. As I began to pray in tongues the goiter instantaneously miraculously disappeared. Wonder filled us all as we witnessed God fulfilling His word as promised.

At the same time God had taught me two very valuable lessons.

1) It was not my faith that produced the miracle but the "faith of Christ" which was lodged in my spirit by the indwelling presence of God the Holy Ghost.

2) The doubt and unbelief of my carnal mind offended the Holy Ghost and worked against the miraculous power of God – without faith it is impossible to please God.

Doubt and unbelief can rob a person of healing and prosperity and all the blessings freely provided in the atonement in Christ Jesus our Lord. Doubt and unbelief offends and frustrates the Lord and stops Him fulfilling His promises and purposes.

The people of that Stone Age village were left in no doubt that Jesus Christ was the living God. No idol could do what they had just witnessed with their own eyes. When Jesus was on earth He healed all who came to Him. He never refused anyone and healed people of all kinds of diseases. Jesus is the same yesterday, today and forever. All he needs now are channels that will work with Him, who believe that he has the miraculous ability to fulfil the promises of his word. Another woman approached me pointing to her goiter. This time all doubt and unbelief was banished from my mind and the goiter instantly disappeared. I rebuked and cast off the spirit of fever and temperatures immediately began to drop. Skin diseases were instantly drying up before our eyes, pains in joints and backs that had spent a lifetime bent over planting and harvesting rice, were instantly healed.

Out of the crowd a little boy came hobbling towards me, crippled by some disease in his legs. He had seen the other miracles and with a child's faith expected to be made normal. Sitting him on the ground I took his feet in my hands and could see that one leg was stunted and withered and was inches shorter than the good leg. Having rebuked and cast out the evil spirit of infirmity I prayed in tongues which released the miraculous power of the Holy Ghost into the situation. The crippled leg lengthened and straightened out until both heels met. With wide eyed wonder he jumped to his feet and looked at his new leg. In three bounds he was gone, shouting at the top of his voice with great excitement and joy, as he went to show off his new leg to his parents. It was the most memorable day of my life!

I sank to my knees with arms raised in the air and praised the Lord for His amazing grace, unconditional agape love and miraculous power. I praised Him that the dry dead bones were no longer dead but had become His dwelling place. I thanked Him for proving Himself to be the one true Holy God, who watches over His word to perform it.

Pastor Teckney would continue the work by sending a Pastor to live with the people and guide them along the narrow road. Pastor Teckney was a very happy man. The events of that meeting revived and strengthened his resolve to obey the Great Commission in its entirety. He confessed that his prayers for the headhunting tribes people had become dry and repetitive over the years, but the joy he experienced that night to see his prayers answered filled him with holy awe.

Chapter Eight

The eyes of the Lord run to and fro about the earth looking for lost sinners who are responding to His grace. No mountain is too high, no valley too deep, no forest too thick for His amazing grace and unconditional love to penetrate. His sight rested on a place called Lewan situated in a mountainous jungle area. My traveling companions and interpreter were Pastor E. Padua, his wife and sister in law, and young men of their Fellowship who humbly volunteered to be our baggage boys. There were no roads into this hidden little paradise, so it was a case of pressing on through well-beaten jungle tracks. The trees around us were tall and provided shade from the merciless sun. Occasionally we heard the chatter of monkeys, who were wise enough to keep at a safe distance, knowing that too much curiosity could lead them to the cooking pot. The trees were many and varied, and I was beginning to recognize the banana tree with its paddle shaped leaves, and mangos hung in the branches high above our heads. I tasted my first pomelo plucked straight from the tree. It is a citrus fruit similar to a grapefruit, and deliciously refreshing, if one is blessed enough to pluck a sweet one. The first pomelo I tasted was so sour that it made my taste buds do a wild dance.

Coconuts grew in abundance far above our heads, "Do you have to wait until the coconuts are ripe, and fall to the ground, before they can be harvested?" I asked my companions. "No, we Filipinos can scale the tree and cut them down." I must have looked a bit unbelieving, so the Pastor called one of young men who was carrying the baggage, to scale the tree and cut down some coconuts. I was amazed, he literally walked up that long straight tree using his hands and feet, whilst his body took on the shape of a horizontal V. Having reached the top he began to hack off coconuts with a big knife carried in his belt. He gave a loud shout, we all stepped backwards, and coconuts began to hit the ground with great thuds. It was an astonishing feat, and three quarters of the way down he let go the tree and jumped.

We sat around singing praises to the Lord, whilst the men were preparing the coconuts. A hole was cut in the center and I drank the coconut milk straight from the shell. It had a delicate thirst-quenching flavor. Then we indulged ourselves in the white meaty pith. One could live in this particular area on what was growing wild by God's provision, which was a completely different scene from the Stone Age village we had left behind. The curse of disease and poverty there due to the sin of idolatry had been broken by God's amazing grace, and now the people could look forward to the blessings of God to change their circumstances.

The hike was long and arduous, but pleasant compared to the previous one up to the Stone Age village. The purpose of this visit was three fold, to encourage and revive the Pastor and the saints, and extend Christ's body by holding outreach meetings, and to reach out to unbelievers. The Pastor and the believers were delighted and overjoyed by our surprise visit, and warmly greeted us with embraces, in the loving way of Filipinos. Sister Carmen was a beautiful handmaiden of the Lord. She had submitted her will in obedience to the will of God, and chose to live in this remote mountain settlement deep in the jungle, as under-shepherd of Christ's flock.

God's presence was almost tangible in this secluded

jungle village, and every tree was laden with His abundance of fruit and rich foliage. Of course they had no electricity or water on tap, yet I was able to have a daily shower, which was a tremendous blessing. Sunset was my favorite time of the day, around five thirty, as the heavens above changed from tropical blue to scarlet and purple. I would make my way to a secluded spring which cascaded down the mountain side. My Filipino brethren had created a lovely remedy. A piece of hollowed bamboo was placed in such a way that the cascading water ran along the bamboo pipe to form a shower of fresh clean water, which ran into a pool below. The setting sun appeared as a flaming ball of fire in the heavens above, only to disappear a few seconds later. Then the curtain of darkness was pulled across the sky. A host of fire flies gathered in the branches all around the pool, their reflection in the water looked like cool drops of pure crystallized silver. It thrilled my soul to experience such a glorious sight. I stood fascinated, almost captivated, watching the little lights dancing around me and above my head. Amid the spectacular sight of many twinkling fireflies, I showered, dressed and prepared for the evening meetings. I could have remained for hours, basking in the cool water, watching the dancing, twinkling little lights. Time forced me to drag myself away from the beauty, and the presence of God in that secluded spot.

There were no dentists or doctors in the near vicinity. The believers walked in Covenant relationship with the holy one of Israel, and believed that they were redeemed from the curse of the law. They received their health, strength, provisions and eternal life by faith, as they ate the bread at the Covenant Table. The bread is the spiritual substance of the Lord's body, broken for us when He endured the lashes of the scourge, to redeem us from the curse of the law. Sickness, pain, disease, suffering, poverty and eternal damnation is the curse of the law. Jesus bore the stripes to set us free. (Galatians 3:13) As they drank from the cup of the Covenant they received by faith, forgiveness for sin, and clothed themselves in the robe of Christ's imputed righteousness.

Unbelievers went to the witchdoctor, but his potions and remedies made people worse rather than better. In desperation they eventually came to Pastor Carmen, who taught them God's word. As they grew in godly knowledge, and responded to God's grace and accepted Jesus as their sin bearer and sacrificial Lamb, she laid hands on them, rebuked the spirits of infirmity, and prayed the prayer of faith. If they believed, they were healed according to the promise that Christ Jesus has redeemed us from the curse of the law. There were no spectacular miracles in Lewan, as the believers were living in divine health according to the provisions of the everlasting Covenant.

During the daytime we often visited families who lived too far from the village to regularly attend the services on Sundays. These families had become believers through Carmen's house visiting ministry. She faithfully tramped through the jungle in high temperatures, and served each believing household with the bread and wine, the emblems of the everlasting Covenant. She kept the sheep revived and ever mindful of their Covenant relationship with the Lord. Returning from one such house visit, over-heated and running with perspiration, we came to a delightful pool in a most unexpected place. The cool, clear depth was an irresistible temptation. We all headed for the water fully dressed. It was a glorious feeling to be immersed in water, after the hike and heat of the tropical sun. As we swam around Carmen said, "This is the baptismal pool that the Lord has provided for us." It was a unique setting, obviously God's provision, as one would not expect to find such a beautiful pool in the middle of a mountainous jungle area. "Praise the Lord, who provides all the needs for His Covenant keeping children." was my reply.

The heavens were declaring that sunset was on its way, "We must head for home, before darkness falls." Carmen told us. Reluctantly leaving the refreshing water, I stretched out my hand to grasp a rock in order to pull my self up out of the water. A sharp pain shot through the flesh of my third finger and I jerked my hand away swiftly, to see blood flowing from quite a deep cut. As I got out of the water with the blood running down my arm, Carmen was quickly by my side, "What happened?"

"I cut my finger on a sharp rock as I got out of the pool. Please join me in the prayer of faith and agreement. 'Father in heaven, I ask in Jesus name, please miraculously draw the flesh together, and heal this wound by the power of the Holy Ghost.'" I squeezed the finger tightly with my other hand, as we prayed in tongues. I continued praying in the Holy Ghost and squeezing the wound together, as I walked back to the pool, swished my hand in the water to remove the blood from my hand and arm. I then looked at my finger. It was a miracle. The wound had closed, only a hairline mark could be traced where the flesh had miraculously joined together. I presented my finger to Susan for inspection and she shouted, "Hallelujah!"

The day came when my companions announced that they had to get back to Baguio, and would be leaving the following morning, "What about you Sister Chapman, have you any plans?"

"Yes, Pastor Calamoing invited me to go to Dagupan." This meant that we would be traveling in opposite directions when we arrived at the highway. I was very sad to leave this wonderful little haven and say goodbye to Carmen and the brethren. I was also sad to say farewell to

Pastor Padua and his company, as they boarded the jeepney bound for Baguio. There I was, all alone, a foreigner in a foreign land, standing by the roadside waiting for a jeep to come along and pick me up. God's timing is always perfect. I did not have to wait long, but was amazed by the sight that came hurtling down the road in my direction. The vehicle was not just overloaded, it was crammed full and overflowing. People were standing on the bumper and step and hanging on to the rail. The roof was jam-packed with sacks of wares, baggage and people. The vehicle looked submerged under a sea of bodies and baggage.

My heart sank. I was convinced that the driver would not stop and pick me up. To my amazement and great relief the driver did stop. Another thing I was finding out was that Filipino men have a godly respect for women. The driver would not leave a woman stranded on the road side all alone. A cheerful young man got up from his seat, made a space for my luggage, and I settled down in his seat with a big "Thank you." His response, "You are welcome, Ma'am." My good mannered kind friend latched himself on to the vehicle, with one hand holding the rail, and one foot on the step into the jeep, in the same manner as other passengers who were hitching a lift. The jeepney took off creaking under its massive load. Another nine stone had just crawled on board. We eventually came to a market town, which was the destination of many of the mountain people. There, they would be able sell their sacks of wares and the remainder of the journey was much less cramped.

I was tired, dirty and weary when the driver finally announced that we had arrived in Pangasinan. My destination was a place named Bliss, which was situated by the seashore, where Pastor and Mrs. Calamoing ran a mission and Bible Training school. The Pastor had invited me to visit them when I met with him at the mission in San

Fernando, soon after my arrival in the country. They had no idea when I would turn up, so my arrival on their campus was an unexpected surprise. Regardless of that, I received the warmest welcome. Immediately Mrs. Calamoing gave instructions to her family to prepare a room for me. She knew and understood the hardship I endured sleeping on bamboo floors, and willingly gave up her mattress, which was the only one they possessed, so that I would enjoy the pleasure of a soft bed during my stay with them. Such is the hospitality and unselfish nature of Filipinos.

The sea was like a millpond, and gently lapped a stretch of beautiful white sand along the coastline. The only problem was the blazing sun, which made it impossible for a white skinned person to swim when the sun was high in the sky. So I enjoyed the blessing of swimming early every morning.

The Pastor arranged outreach meetings in outlying villages along the coast. God worked with us, as I preached the Gospel, drawing lost sinners to Himself by His amazing grace. I laid hands on the sick and cast out spirits of infirmity, and people were healed and set free from fevers and all kinds of ailments. One memorable miracle that particular week was a man who had suffered a stroke ten years previously. The stroke had left one side of his face paralyzed, which was hideously disfiguring his facial appearance. Addressing the paralytic spirit, I bound it in spiritual chains and commanded it to loose its hold of the man, in the name of Jesus Christ of Nazareth. Laying my hands on his face, I prayed in Holy Ghost tongues, and God miraculously did what was necessary to bring the man's body into line with that which Jesus stripes had freely provided for him. When I removed my hands his face was normal, as was his speech. He raised his hands in the air and praised and thanked God for his miracle, with tears of thanksgiving and joy streaming down his cheeks. His great joy was the fact that his grandchildren would no longer cower away from him in fear.

Our schedule the next day was to a small island named Pugarao. We made our way over the water in a wooden boat driven by a small engine. Within ten minutes of being on the island, I began to shake and felt desperately ill. It was as though every ounce of energy had been drained from my body. My head swam with dizziness, and I knew that I would collapse if I did not sit down. According to my companions I looked ghastly, my face was drained of all color. My companions took an arm either side of me, to support and help bear the weight of my body and steered me towards a hammock, which was tied in the shade between two coconut trees. Pastor Calamoing was at my side, "Sister Chapman, what you are experiencing is a direct satanic attack. We have been praying for the inhabitants of this island for many years. Every time we have tried to evangelize the people on this island, we have met with the same attack as you are now experiencing. There are approximately 150 people living here, and five different cults operate on this island alone. The people's lives are dominated by witchcraft, voodoo and superstition and spiritism."

Lying on the hammock feeling worse with every passing second, hearing the Pastor's words had been informative, but not in the slightest bit encouraging. I was already sensing the spiritual oppression in the heavy, uneasy atmosphere of the island. The thought came to mind, "Ask your companions to help you back to the boat and leave this place as fast as possible." I was well aware of the fact that other voices could speak to me, the devils agents could plant thoughts into the mind, and I realized that the enemy wanted me off this island fast. As I fought the nausea and dizziness, the Holy Ghost spoke within me, "I have given you authority to trample on snakes and scorpions and to overcome all the power of the enemy, and nothing will harm you". (Luke 10:19) The voice that told me to, "leave the island fast" spoke to my mind, not in an audible voice, but rather was impressed on my mind. When God speaks to us, it is the Holy Ghost communicating to our spirit. It is not an audible voice, but a strong impression in my innermost being. Raising my hand I waved and beckoned the Pastor to come to me, "I have been praying for you, are you beginning to feel better?"

"We need to stand together, and pray the prayer of faith and agreement. Please call the rest of our team and ask them to lay hands on me, and agree with my prayer."

With a dozen hands laid on me I began to pray, "I address you evil spirit of infirmity that is attacking my body, you have no legal right near me, I am cleansed and accepted as holy and righteous through faith in Christ's redeeming blood. Jesus has redeemed me from the curse of the law. Therefore you have no legal right to attack my body with weakness, dizziness and nausea. In the name of Jesus Christ of Nazareth I tie you up in spiritual chains and render you powerless and ineffective in this attack against me. Loose your hold of me this instant. Father, I ask in Jesus' name, that you send an angel of light, to take the demons that I have just bound, to the waiting place to await the final judgment, to be cast into the lake of fire and brimstone. Thank you, Lord, that I am loosed and set free. As we pray in the power of the Holy Ghost, I will receive full strength and health to my body, as I was healed by the Lord's stripes." After a time of praying in the power of the Holy Ghost, I got up from the hammock perfectly healed.

God's word is truth, and when we apply it with

unwavering faith it cannot fail us. The pastor was right, we were facing a head-on collision with the forces of darkness. Sickness and disease is normally a result of the curse of the law, working against those who do not understand or believe that Christ has redeemed us from the curse of the law. I know my standing in Christ Jesus, therefore the enemy had no legal authority to bring me under the curse of the law. The devil's only weapon against me was his evil wiles. The forces of darkness had tried to rob me of the healing which Jesus stripes freely purchased and provided for me. When on earth, Jesus went about doing good, healing all who were oppressed of the devil. (Acts 10:38) A study of the gospels reveals that ninety percent of Jesus earthly ministry revolved around casting out demons and healing the sick.

The devil and his oppressing evil spirit was under my feet, through faith in the all powerful name of the Lord Jesus Christ, and I proved it by getting up off that hammock to fulfill the planned mission to the island. As we walked around the island inviting every one to attend the meeting that night, I felt fit, healthy and strong, and ready for any challenge that the devil and his agents may put in our way. Facing the truth I realized that demons are merely fallen angels who were cast out of heaven. Jesus' mission to earth was to 'destroy the works of the devil', and set us free from the curse of the law. Jesus said, "Go in my name and cast out devils." Jesus gave believers the power of attorney to use His name, to execute power over the evil works of the devil. In the name of the Lord Jesus Christ we have the victory.

As usual I was followed around the island by a band of some thirty children, fascinated by my white skin and brown hair. Eventually, some became bold enough to hold my hand as we walked on. Darkness had fallen by the time we completed our round of the island and were ready to begin the service. Some one had lent us a tillie lamp, very similar to the one my mother used when I was a child. The lamp had a mantle and wick steeped in paraffin, and was much more effective than a kerosene lamp. The tillie lamp was hung from a hook fixed to a rafter, lowered by a piece of rope to give me maximum light to read from the Bible. The service commenced with praises to the Lord. Suddenly the lamp began to sway about in an alarming manner, blinked a few times as if it had run out of paraffin and then went out, plunging the meeting into sudden darkness. The owner assured us that he had filled it before presenting it to the Pastor, "It has not run out of paraffin." stated Pastor Calamoing. The praising stopped while the lamp was relit and attached to the rope in its original position. Our musician started strumming on the guitar, and we again began singing praises to the God of our Salvation. Then the lamp started dancing about, swinging to and fro above my head, blinked a few times and for the second time we were plunged into darkness. The reason for the lamp's antics were inexplicable as there was no wind or draught to interfere with it. Then it happened a third time, and our praises ceased as we were thrust into darkness yet again. I could sense that people were feeling uneasy, even frightened, the atmosphere was weird, spooky, and the events unexplainable. After the third relighting, I decided to get on with preaching God's word. Before I got to the end of the first verse the lamp once again began to act as if it had a mind of its own. It swung to and fro wildly above my head. It blinked a few times and again we were plunged into thick blackness. Four times this happened within the space of fifteen minutes and then the following scripture came to my mind.

Ephesians 6:12

For we wrestle not against flesh and blood, but against principalities, against powers, against the rulers of darkness of this world, against spiritual wickedness in high places.

We cannot see into the spirit realm. However we must be aware of the fact that the spirit world is as real as our physical world. Our fight is not against human beings of flesh and blood, but against Satan's army of warring demons, principalities, and powers who rule over this dark world performing spiritual wickedness in high places. Believers have no reason to fear this satanic army. Our enemy was defeated by Christ Jesus two thousand plus years ago and the demons know that they were defeated, and must obey the name of the Lord Jesus Christ. The spirit realm contains more than just evil principalities and powers; it consists also of God's holy angels who remained faithful to God when Lucifer and his rebellious angels were cast out of heaven. I believe that when we bind demons in spiritual chains and render them powerless and ineffective through faith in the power vested in the name of the Lord Jesus Christ, God's Holy angels are there to take those demons to hell, to await the final judgment, when they will be forever banished to the torment of the lake of fire and brimstone.

We could not see the demonic forces that were causing the tillie lamp to wave about in its wild antics. But we saw the effects of what they were doing. Fear is a great tool of the enemy, and the unexplained movement of the lamp and suddenly being plunged into darkness was causing people to be frightened. Through fear, the enemy tried to get the congregation to abandon the meeting. This particular group of wicked spirits overplayed their hand, as I began to see through their wiles. Righteous anger rose within me, as people were fumbling about in the darkness trying to light the lamp. I spoke in a loud clear voice," In the name of the

Lord Jesus Christ of Nazareth, I address you evil demons that are trying to stop this meeting. I tie you up in spiritual chains and render you powerless to interfere further with the progress of this meeting. I command that you leave these premises immediately. It is written you must obey the name of the Lord Jesus Christ. Father in Heaven, I ask that you will dispatch an angel of light to take these demons to the waiting place, to await the final judgment."

I believed that my prayer was being carried out in the spirit realm. The lamp's mantle burst into a bright steady glow, and we began the meeting again with the chorus, "In the name of Jesus we have the victory." We had no further interference, and the devil lost approximately fifty souls that evening, translated out of the kingdom of darkness into the kingdom of God - Christ's body on earth. The incidents of the lamp going out, then burning brightly with no further interference, had a profound effect on the assembled company, and proved to them that the name of the Lord Jesus Christ is the name above all names. All things work together for good for those who love God, and are called according to his purposes.

The Pastor and his companions got the people to renounce the pagan cults they had been involved with, and then he sent them to me for prayer for deliverance and healing. They were all under the curse of the law, suffering different kinds of sickness and disease. It would have taken all night to pray for them individually. I raised my hands in the air and prayed as follows, "Now that you have renounced the satanic cults you have been involved with, and responded to God's grace by accepting Jesus Christ as the only Saviour of sinners, I address every demon that has been deceiving you, and tie them up in spiritual chains and command them to leave you, now, in the name of the Lord Jesus Christ. Christ has redeemed you from the curse of the law, therefore no sickness, pain or disease has any legal hold over you. In the name of the Lord Jesus Christ I tie up every spirit of pain and infirmity in spiritual chains, and render you powerless, and command you to leave their bodies now, take your symptoms and flee to the waiting place to await the final judgment." I moved among the people, laying hands on them praying in the Holy Ghost. Tears of joy and thanksgiving was seen and heard all around the room. Every one without exception was instantly and totally healed.

All miracles are memorable, but the most amazing miracle we witnessed that evening was of a woman who had suffered a stroke which had left her paralyzed down her right side. She was able to move her limbs for the first time in years, and ended up jumping and dancing with joy as she thanked the Lord for setting her free.

At the end of the meeting we were asked by a new convert if we would accompany her to her home, to pray for her grandfather who was at the point of death, dying of a hereditary disease. The Lord Jesus Christ has redeemed believers from the curse of the law, which includes all hereditary diseases. When a person dies of a hereditary disease, the demon that caused the symptoms, leaves the dead body and take up residence in another living body, thus hereditary diseases pass from one generation to another. However they can only pass to those who are under the curse of the law. They have no authority to oppress those who know their standing in Christ Jesus, and are protected by the blood of the Covenant. The devil may try out his evil wiles on us, but we have authority over the demons in the name of the Lord Jesus Christ. Arriving at a small bamboo dwelling house, we found the grandfather lying on the wooden floor. He was such a sad sight. He was a skeleton of skin and bone, even breathing had become a hard laborious task for him. My heart filled with compassion for him, and I thought he was unconscious as he did not seem to be aware of our presence. Taking hold of his old bony hand, I simply cried out in my heavenly language, which released the Holy Ghost to reach into his spirit and reveal Jesus to him. Something happened as he opened his eyes and nodded his head. Then he remained motionless. I addressed the evil spirit that had passed to him at his father's death. "I address you hereditary demon of disease and tie you up in spiritual chains, and render you powerless to pass to another member of this family. I command you to loose your hold of this body now, in the name of the Lord Jesus Christ of Nazareth. Father in Heaven, please send an angel of light to take this hereditary demon of disease to the waiting place, to await the final judgment, so that it cannot corrupt another human body on earth. Amen."

On the way back to our little craft we thanked God that the angels in heaven were rejoicing over those who had been saved and regenerated by the indwelling Holy Ghost. All things work together for good, for those who love God, and are called according to His purposes. On our way back to the mainland by the light of the moon, we discussed how the devil's attack on my physical body, and the wild antics of the dancing lamp, worked for good, and had revealed to the people that the name of our Lord truly was the most powerful name in the universe.

One of the Bible students who had accompanied us to the island would be graduating in a few month's time. She approached Pastor Calamoing and said that she felt led of the Lord to go and live on the island, and would pastor the new sheep. He was delighted. His prayer concerning who would continue the work had been answered. The Lord had everything under his control and leading.

I was now running out of ready cash and needed to get back to the bank in San Fernando to see if a transfer had arrived. So I planned to leave the following Monday. Saying goodbye to the brethren was never easy, but was becoming a common occurrence in my itinerant life style.

Chapter Nine

B ack at the mission in San Fernando, I rested and reflected on the ways in which God had used me as an instrument of His saving and healing power, which filled me with wondrous joy. Nothing in this world could compare with following in His will, and being a channel of His blessing. I went to bed in perfectly good health, but woke to find myself in Lorma hospital, with no knowledge of how I got there. My first realization that things were not as they should be was finding myself in a hospital bed wired to a drip. A white clad nurse was smiling down at me, "Why am I here?"

"We nearly lost you, you have typhoid fever."

Then I must have drifted back into unconsciousness. Yet I was aware of the fact that my body was being submerged in a bath of iced water. At other times I was aware that my body felt as though it was in a furnace. I was burning up with a fever which threatened to melt my brain. I had quick flashes of what was happening to me, as I fell in and out of delirium. For five days I was under observation in a critical condition. It truly was a terrible experience. One moment I was burning up, as if my body was on fire, my next recollection would be of shaking and shivering. My entire body shook so violently that every muscle and sinew felt as if it were being torn apart. I said what I thought to be my final prayer, expecting at any moment to pass through the valley of the shadow of death as my spirit was released from the veil of flesh. I would see Jesus face-to-face, and live with Him forever in His perfect world.

Then suddenly my mind became curiously lucid and I

was aware of the fact that I was in hospital, all alone in a room, yet I was not alone. I could sense God's awesome presence fill the room. For the first time I heard the audible voice of Almighty God, "YOU MUST GIVE THE MESSAGE TO THE CHURCH!" I held my breath in absolute awe and incredulity. Once more the authoritative yet gentle voice of God resounded in my ears. "YOU MUST GIVE THE MESSAGE TO THE CHURCH!"

As I lay there, pondering on this amazing thing that had just happened, an overwhelming desire for 'water,' suddenly swept over me. I had to get up and take a step of faith. Without faith it is impossible to please God. I struggled out of that death bed, and stumbled across the floor, half walking half crawling, and made my way to the shower in the far corner. With what felt like my last ounce of energy, I turned on the tap, and then collapsed on the floor with the water pouring over my body. It was the act of faith that was needed to release the power of the Holy Ghost into my sick body. Faith moves God to move on our behalf. With the water washing over my body, I finally had the strength to rise to my feet. Raising my hands in the air, I began to praise and worship the Lord. The running water reminded me of God's word, and I remembered the scripture, "He sent His word and healed them!" I somehow had a knowing that the water I really needed was more knowledge of God's word, not the water that was pouring over me in the shower.

"Thank you, Lord. By your stripes I am healed." The healing which Jesus' stripes freely provided for us shot through my body from the top of my head to the tips of my toes. Miraculously and instantaneously my body came into line with God's word. The fever was gone. The curse of typhoid was lifted from me. I was strong and healthy, healed by the divine health which Jesus stripes freely purchased and provided for us. I dried my body and dressed, and signed out of the hospital, with the promise to settle my bill the following day. The hospital staff were amazed. I never looked back. That traumatic event happened in the year 1980. Throughout the past twenty-seven years, I have not even once consulted a doctor or been hospitalized. God proved to me that His word is all-sufficient and that He and He alone is the Great Physician.

However, that does not mean to say that I have not faced enemy attack, especially in the early days of my calling when my mind was being renewed and brought into harmony with God's word. The next battle I faced was a lump that appeared under my left arm. I bound the enemy and commanded the spirit of infirmity to depart from my body in the name of the Lord Jesus Christ. Nothing changed, the lump remained, but the word of God admonishes believers to stand our ground by faith, and wholeheartedly trust in the promises of our Father's word. We need God's armour to withstand in trying times, and having done all we can we must stand firm in faith, believing in the complete atonement in Jesus Christ.

Ephesians 6:13

Wherefore take unto you the whole armour of God, that ye may be able to withstand in the evil day, and having done all, to STAND.

To walk in the victory that Jesus has freely provided for us we must be clothed in God's armour. I did what was necessary to set myself free from a spirit of infirmity through faith in the name of the Lord Jesus Christ. Then I had to stand my ground by faith, believing that I was healed by the Lord's stripes regardless of the evidence of my natural senses - what I felt and saw. The natural truth and fact of the matter was I had a painful lump under my arm. Symptoms dictate to us our circumstances - you are sick, you have an incurable disease, you are broke and have no money, you have high blood pressure etc. The devil, the world view and our carnal sense knowledge would have us believe that symptoms as revealed by sense knowledge are truth. The doctor may tell a person that the tests prove they have an incurable disease. This is a natural fact. Yet there is a spiritual truth, which teaches, "We were healed by the Lords stripes." We have to stand our ground by faith, believing and confessing God's word. God's word is a living word, which carries His faith, and the miraculous ability to create that which He has promised. A person may be broke and have no money – this is a natural fact. Yet there is a spiritual truth which teaches that God has promised to provide all our needs according to His riches in glory, by Christ Jesus. Therefore we have to stand our ground by faith, believing for the financial blessing to be made manifest according to God's promise. We as individuals have to make the decision. We have to decide whether to believe the natural circumstances or the spiritual truth.

I determined to stand by faith and believe the spiritual truth. I was healed by the Lord's stripes. I did not deny the symptoms. It would be untrue to say that I did not have a painful lump under my arm. However it was only a natural symptom, which I looked upon as a temporary thing. The spiritual truth is far greater - Jesus and His word is truth. Natural symptoms cannot change the truth, but when we apply the truth of God's word with unwavering faith, the truth causes the symptoms to disappear. I applied the truth to my symptoms (painful lump under my arm) on a regular basis, laying my hand on the lump daily or when it was paining me, and spoke the spiritual truth. "I am healed by the Lords stripes, and I thank you Lord that my body is coming into line with your word. This lump is only a temporary thing." A Biblical principle that never fails is that everyone gets what they believe in their heart and speak with their mouth. This truth is revealed in Mark 11:22-24. According to Proverbs 18:21 – Death and life are in the power of the tongue.

When we feed on the truth by planting God's word in our hearts, wholeheartedly believe the truth, as well as speak the truth, the truth changes the natural circumstances. One morning approximately one month after the growth appeared, I was having my shower, and as I washed under my arm realization hit me. The lump was gone. "Hallelujah! Thank you Lord. I praise you, you are the God of truth, and your word carries your faith and miraculous ability to reproduce itself." Yet I continued to have an unanswered question in my heart. Jesus has redeemed us from the curse of the law, so why was I inflicted with typhoid fever which is a killer disease? Why had I suffered this lump under my arm? I was living a holy life. I had given up smoking and was conforming to the accepted Christian standards. I was not aware of any hidden sin in my life. It was not unbelief, because I believed with all my heart that I was healed by the Lord's stripes.

Some months later I found myself in another battle. I had a lump on my left breast. The first thing I had to overcome was fear, and stood on the scripture. "God has not given me the spirit of fear, but of love, and power and a sound mind." I rebuked and cast out the spirit of fear, and commanded the spirit of infirmity which had caused the lump on my breast to depart from me, through faith in the in the all powerful name of our Lord Jesus. I received God's peace, and again stood on the word. "By the Lord's stripes I am healed." Once again I was asking the question. Jesus has redeemed me from the curse of the law – sickness, pain, disease, poverty and the second death, why did I keep having these recurring physical problems? I did not go to a doctor, but determined to prove God's word. "Christ has redeemed us from the curse of the law. By His stripes I was healed." I would not let go. If God's word did not work for me, how could I preach it with conviction? By the grace of God I got the victory, and the lump disappeared as well as the stabbing pains. Yet, my question remained unanswered.

I had forgiven every one who had hurt me. I was not harboring resentment, bitterness or unforgiveness in my heart. I was living a holy life, separated from the world. I had no unconfessed sin. I did not smoke or drink. I read my bible daily, I was doing all that I knew possible to remain in right standing with God. Where was I going wrong? I took the easy way out and blamed the devil! The typhoid fever, the lump under my arm, the lump on my breast, it had all been an attack of the devil, who had tried to rob me of the health which Jesus' stripes had freely provided for me. Some months later I found myself in another war zone. I had to battle my way through arthritic pains in my knees. It really hurt, and I was in constant pain, so I killed the pain with pain relief tablets. Finally I got the victory by standing on the word and regularly eating and drinking the bread and wine at the Covenant Table, whereby I established and reaffirmed my side of the Covenant agreement by faith. God's mercy and grace always came through for me, as I stood on His word with unwavering faith.

I had to face the facts. It is written, "Christ has redeemed us from the curse of the Law." (Gal 3:13). If the devil was responsible for making me sick, it meant that his power was greater than the atonement in Christ's stripes. This is most definitely not the case, because Jesus came into our world to set us free from the power of sin, Thus, He destroyed the works of the devil. Jesus perfectly accomplished that which he came to do on our behalf. So I continued to seek the Lord for understanding concerning why I found myself in a situation where I was being judged by the Law, under the curse of symptoms of disease.

Cynthia is a deacon at Covenant Keepers, who has often prayed the prayer of faith and agreement with me, when ministering to the sick.. It was reported to me one morning that she was rushed into the local hospital in Bacnotan, during the night. I immediately went to pray for her, and was shocked by her appearance. Overnight she had aged twenty years. I could hardly believe that this was our Cynthia. Her eyes were sunken into her head, and she had lost stones in weight overnight. It was unbelievable! "What happened to you Cynthia?"

"It started with vomiting and diarrhea. I feel as if I am going to die."

I thought to myself, "She looks like she is dying", but did not say those words. Laying hands on her, I cast the demons of infirmity off her in the all-powerful name of the Lord Jesus Christ, and prayed for her healing. Next day, I was informed that she had been moved to another hospital in San Fernando. This was a serious matter. I remembered her words, "I feel as if I am going to die." The only reason she would be moved to the City hospital, would be that the district hospital could not handle her case. Upon hearing this latest news I immediately headed out to visit her. Sitting by her bedside, she said, "They gave me a scan and the tests reveal that I have angina." She knew the healing scriptures, she knew that she was healed by the Lord's stripes. Taking a deep breath, I decided that there was no room for compromise. She was under demonic oppression, under the curse of the law. Why was she suffering under the curse of the law, when the scriptures reveal, "Christ has redeemed us from the curse of the law?"

Once again I blamed the devil for trying to rob her of the healing which Jesus' stripes had freely provided for her.

I took authority over the oppressing demons and loosed her in the name of our Lord Jesus. "Cynthia, this is just an attack of the devil, you have to make a decision, you can choose to accept angina and exalt the doctor's report above the word of God. Or you can renounce the doctor's report and believe the report of the Great Physician who has declared, "By my stripes you were healed."

Then the thought came to my mind, "Can you not see that she is a very sick woman, how can you talk to her like this, giving her an ultimatum, she is too sick to make such a decision."

"Get out of my mind, devil. I refuse to listen to you." Looking into Cynthia's eyes, I could see she needed reassurance. "Cynthia, you cannot exalt the doctor's report above God's word." She nodded her head, and I led her in a prayer to renounce angina, and stand firm on the report of the Great Physician who said, "By my stripes you were healed!" She was due for another scan that afternoon, so we prayed the prayer of faith and agreement together. "Heavenly Father, I thank you that Cynthia was healed by the Lord's stripes, and that her body is coming into line with your word, and will soon be home, I forbid any demon to interfere with the scan report, and I ask that you dispatch an angel of light to watch over her, and keep her safe from further demonic attack, in the mighty name of Jesus Christ."

The following day as I walked towards her bedside she looked so well, the Cynthia that I knew and loved was looking her normal self. I raised my arms and said, "Thank you Lord, praise your holy name for answered prayers."

"The second scans showed no sign of angina, the doctors are puzzled, so they are giving me another scan this afternoon." said Cynthia.

"Praise the Lord!"

Before leaving her I prayed with her again. I thanked God that his angel was guarding over her, and just to be sure I forbade any demons to interfere with the third scan result, in Christ's name. The following day I was back at her bedside. The third scan showed no sign of angina. The doctors compared the first scan with the later two scans, and could give no explanation as to why the first scan was so different from the penultimate and third scan. They decided to give her a fourth scan to settle the matter. The fourth scan was clear. We applied truth to the circumstances, and the facts changed. She was home within five days, and has had no further trouble.

Some time afterwards I said to Cynthia, "You know, and believe, that Christ has redeemed us from the curse of the law. Why do you think the curse was able to work against you?"

"My heart was hurting because of gossip and backstabbing in our neighborhood. They had no right to criticize me. When I compared my righteous life style with theirs, I saw that they are they were the ones who were living in sin."

"So unforgiveness was the cause of the trouble!"

"No, I took them to the Lord and forgave them, before I was sick."

I concluded that self-righteousness was the problem. She saw herself as being more righteous than her neighbors. She was looking at her righteous life style, talking about her own righteousness, being superior to that of her neighbors.

"Do you believe that your righteous life style gives you right standing with God?" I asked her. I think realization of the truth hit us both at the same moment. The only righteousness that God accepts is perfect righteousness, which neither she, nor I, nor her neighbors possessed. The only way anyone can possess perfect righteousness, which keeps us protected from the curse of the law, is to be clothed in Christ's imputed righteousness, by faith in the promises of God's word.

"Cynthia, there is none righteous in our flesh. We cannot boast about our righteous life style, because it falls short of the perfect righteousness which God requires and accepts. The blackened pot was talking to the blackened kettle. Without being clothed in Christ's perfect imputed righteousness by faith none can escape the judgment of the Law. The judgment of the Law brings one under the curse of the law, sickness, suffering, disease poverty and the second death. Unbelievers will face the second death – not because of their sins. The price of sin is fully paid. The law will judge and condemn them for rejecting Jesus atonement on their behalf."

Both Cynthia and I believed that the death and blood of Jesus gave us right standing with God. But we had been seduced into mixing grace and faith with our good works. I came to realize that the reason that the curse was able to work against us was because of our self-righteousness. I got on my knees and thanked God for His amazing mercy and grace, which had brought us both through the trials of being judged by the Law. Without realizing, I had moved away from total trust in the death and blood of the atonement in Christ for my right standing with God. Therefore I came under the judgment of the Law. If we mix grace and faith with our good works and living a holy life, we will be conforming to a law of works, we will be judged by the law, and so come under the curse of the Law, because we have all broken the Law. If we slip back into 'works and law keeping' and mix our righteous efforts with grace and faith for right standing with God, that means we are trusting in our good living standards and efforts for justification - trusting in our own righteousness, which is dead works or filthy rags in God's sight.

When I rededicated my life to the Lord, and obeyed His call to give up my employment and sell all that I owned, I was looked upon as a carnal Christian, who could not possibly be called of God because I was a smoker. This was the attitude of my brethren. I realized that I would have to comply with the law of works to be accepted by them. This was also the situation with the brethren in the Philippines. I determined to give up smoking and comply with the New Testament law of works taught and believed by everyone I had come into fellowship with since rededicating my life to full time service in the Lord's vineyard.

Now I was beginning to understand why I had gone through the various battles with my physical health. I came to understand that I was being judged by the Law. The curse was working against me. I had unwittingly moved my position of belief, and was no longer wholeheartedly trusting in Christ's imputed righteousness for total acceptance with God. I had got into a mindset whereby I was going about establishing my own righteousness, by complying with a law of works in order to be accepted.

Romans 10: 3-5

For they being ignorant of God's righteousness, and going about to establish their own righteousness, have not submitted themselves unto the righteousness of God.

I was no longer wholeheartedly submitting to the righteousness of God, but mixing grace, faith and religious law-keeping. This caused me to fall from grace, and so I was judged by the Law, and came under the curse of the Law.

Philippians 3: 9

And be found in him, not having mine own righteousness, which is of the law, but that which is through the faith of Christ.

The righteousness which is of God by faith.

I was grieved in my heart to realize that I had moved from my position of heart belief and had been trusting in my own righteousness, by conforming to a New Testament law of works. My eyes were opened. All self-righteousness is dead works and as filthy rags, in God's sight. Right standing with God cannot be accomplished by our obedience to a law of works. We have failed, we sin, and we are far from perfect, so we cannot be justified and redeemed from the judgment of the Law if we live by a law of works. The Lord Jesus said, "Except your righteousness shall exceed the righteousness of the scribes and Pharisees, ye shall in no case enter the kingdom of heaven." (Mat 5: 20) There is true righteousness provided for us in Jesus Christ which is a complete and perfect righteousness. To mix grace, faith and works, and believe that our outward ordinances and good deeds are able to atone for our sins and give us right standing with God, is trusting in a false gospel. This brings us back under the judgment of the Law, and the curse of the law automatically works against us. This was the reason I suffered typhoid fever, the lump under my arm, the lump on my breast and arthritic knees – because if we trust in our self-righteousness and a law of works, we will be judged by the law, and come under its curse, because we have all broken the Law. Law is Law and grace is grace. We are either under Law or under grace, we cannot mix the two. Christ's sacrificial death and redeeming blood paid the full ransom payment for our sins. His atonement was all-sufficient, He does not need our added good works to give us right standing with God. If we add to the atonement by self-effort, we are saying Christ's atonement was not sufficient for us. We fall from grace and come under the judgment of the law, and find ourselves in a cursed situation.

This sad state of affairs comes about because we are not conforming to the principle that has redeemed us from the curse of the law. This principle is to abide in the true vine, the atonement in our Lord Jesus Christ by faith, and faith alone. We must be clothed by faith in the robe of Christ's imputed righteousness, which His death and redeeming blood freely provided for us. This is the only way we as believers can avoid being judged by the Law, and escape the curse of the Law. Being redeemed from the curse of the law is the gift of God's amazing mercy and grace towards fallen humanity. (Titus 3: 5-6) If we mix or try to add to Christ's atonement by adhering to a religious law of works, we automatically come under the judgment of the law, and are no longer redeemed from the curse of the Law. God will not accept our good living efforts as a plus towards our righteous standing with Him, because it falls short of perfect righteousness.

I praised God for His amazing grace, which had brought me through this deception. I humbled myself before our Lord, renounced my self-righteous efforts to gain favor with the holy one of Israel. I received my forgiveness, and cast off my filthy garment of fig leaves – filthy rags. I received my forgiveness by grace through faith in the redeeming blood of Jesus, and clothed myself with Christ's imputed righteousness as a garment. The Lord Jesus Christ is the Lord of our righteousness. (Jeremiah 23: 6) There is none righteous, no, not one. (Isaiah 64: 6) No sinner can be justified in God's sight by a mixture of faith in Christ's atonement and conforming to any form of law of works, because we have all broken God's law. Therefore we cannot be justified in the sight of God, by obedience to any form of religious law keeping. Believers are justified by God's grace through faith, in the imputed righteousness of Christ, without the deeds of the law - without adhering to any form of law of works. Mankind's obedience to a law of works is his own righteousness – dead works, filthy rags in God's sight. Self-righteousness denies the full sufficiency in the atonement in Christ's death and blood. If righteousness comes by the law of works, then Christ is dead in vain. (Gal 2:21)

Jesus did not come into the world, either to destroy or relax the law of God, but to fulfill the law on behalf of sinners. This required a perfect holy nature and perfect obedience from birth to death. Both were in our Lord Jesus, the Lamb of God. Jesus bore the whole penalty of the Law, (which we should have born because of our sins,) as our sacrificial Lamb and scapegoat. All the requirements of the Law were fulfilled in and by Jesus; all its severities were executed in and upon Him. He thereby magnified the Law given by God the Father at Mount Sinai, and made it honorable. By so doing Jesus redeemed believers from the curses, condemnation and consequences of breaking the law, but He did not abolish or relax the Law. Rather He fulfilled it in our stead.

We have to live by faith in what Jesus atonement freely provided for us, as a gift of God's amazing grace. We are no longer under a Covenant of Law, therefore are not under obedience to any form of law of works. We are under the new better Covenant of Grace, whereby Jesus fulfilled the works on our behalf. We are redeemed from the curse – sickness, pain, suffering, poverty and the second death, providing we conform to the principles that have redeemed us from the curse of the law. This principle is to live by grace through faith in the perfect atonement which Jesus has freely provided for us. And not by trying to help God out by our own acts of obedience and law keeping. The Law continues to stand in its full mandatory, cursing and damning power over all who are not redeemed from its power, by grace through faith in the atonement in Christ Jesus. We can confess with our mouth, "Christ has redeemed me from the curse of the law." That is not sufficient to protect us from the curse of the law. We have to live in the benefits, which the atonement freely provided for us, by grace through faith.

The New Testament gospel does *not* carry a law of obedience. Jesus did not institute New Testament law. By grace are you saved through faith, *not of works* lest any man boast. (Eph 2: 8-9) The gospel of grace is not a gospel of works of law: it carries no law. The requirement is faith in the finished work of the atonement in our Lord Jesus Christ. Acts 20:24 describes the gospel, as the gospel of the grace of God. The gospel of grace reveals the exceeding riches of God's mercy and amazing grace, towards fallen humanity. It is called the gospel of our salvation, which has saved us from the curse of the law, not by works of righteousness which we have done.

Jesus saved us through His works; his suffering the pain and agony of the scourge, by whose stripes we were healed. He died as our substitute sacrificial Lamb, his death paid the full ransom price for all our sins. His holy blood atoned for our sins – without the shedding of blood there is no remission for sin. Therefore there are no works required by New Covenant believers. The requirement is faith in the atoning works of Christ our Saviour. Good works come about as a result of our salvation, but can never be a means of obtaining right standing with God.

Even as a child, I had known and believed that I was redeemed by the precious blood of Jesus, and not by obedience to any form of religious law or works. Unwittingly, I had now been deceived into following 'another gospel' that embraced a law of works, which had brought me under the curse of the law. I had to face the fact that I was no longer conforming to the principle that had redeemed me from the curse. This principle is absolute trust and faith in the atonement in Christ Jesus, not of works lest any man boast.

The penalty for sin was fully paid by Jesus, therefore the consequences of sin, which is the curse of the law, was absolutely completely and totally eliminated. Annulled! Christ has redeemed us from the curse of the law, providing we abide in His atonement by grace through faith. If we add a law of obedience to the gospel of grace, we are perverting so great a salvation, which is strictly based on God's goodness, mercy and grace towards fallen humanity.

The righteousness that keeps believers protected from the curse of the law, and justified in God's sight, is not our own righteousness, but belongs to another, and is therefore imputed righteousness. It is being clothed in Christ's imputed righteousness by faith, which keeps us protected from the curse of the law. When we first believed and accepted Christ as our Saviour, we were dead in trespass and sin. We wholeheartedly believed in the blood of Jesus to cleanse us of all unrighteousness. God accepted us then, just as we were, with all our faults and weaknesses. Now that we are believers, we must beware of being brain washed into believing that we now have to conform to a law of works for right standing with God. Such thinking and believing turns us away from the true way of salvation to 'another gospel', which brings us back under the curse of the law.

We must continue our walk with God in exactly the same way as we started out, by grace through faith. We are still sinners, albeit redeemed sinners. If we say we have no sin, we deceive ourselves, and the truth is not in us. Our flesh continues to have weaknesses and faults, nothing much has changed as far as our mortal flesh is concerned. Jesus' atonement did not remove sin from our mortal flesh. Jesus' atonement paid the penalty for the sins of the world, and redeemed us from the consequences of sin – the curse of the law. Flesh is flesh. It has been contaminated by hereditary sin from Adam. There is a constant warfare within every born again believer, as seen in Romans 7: 14-25.

The imputed righteousness of our Lord Jesus is our life-belt that keeps us in right standing with the holy one of Israel, and protects us from the curse of the law. If we drop our life-belt (Christ's imputed righteousness) we begin to drown, and find ourselves in a situation where we are being judged by the Law, and so come under the curse of the law. When we drop our life-belt we are no longer conforming to the principle that has redeemed us from the curse – total faith and trust in Christ's atonement on our behalf.

The great change that happens to us when we are born again takes place in our spirit.

Our spirit is regenerated by the indwelling Holy Ghost. God is 'in' us. Our spirit has been created a new creature in Christ Jesus, bearing the image and likeness of God. Adam lost the image and likeness of God through his disobedience and rebellion in the Garden of Eden.

God created Adam in His own image – an eternal being.

God created Adam in His own likeness – perfectly holy and righteous.

Our Born again regenerate spirit possesses the eternal life of God, and is perfectly holy and righteous. Our born again spirit cannot sin, because it is born of God.

We are all born into this world bearing a disobedient rebellious sin nature which we inherited from Adam. Adam's sin was imparted to our mortal flesh.

By means of the new birth (regeneration) Christ's

righteousness and eternal life is imparted to our spirit. The reverse of what happened to Adam, when he fell in the garden, happens to our spirit when we are born of God.

Our body of flesh is only our temporary dwelling place, and can move towards only one destiny – death. Death of the physical body opens the door into Glory for our regenerate spirit, which will be clothed in immortality on resurrection day. To preserve our flesh from premature death, and remain on earth as Christ's disciples, to fulfill God's will for our lives, we must be clothed in Christ's imputed righteousness by faith at all times.

All born again believers possess a dual nature, for as long as we reside in our mortal body of flesh. Our flesh possesses an old Adamic nature, which serves the law of sin. Therefore the drive to sin is always present with us. Our regenerate spirit has been regenerated and created a duplicate of Jesus, perfectly holy and righteous possessing eternal life. (See Romans 7, Galatians 5, and 1 John 3). Adam imparted sin and death to our mortal flesh. Christ, the last Adam, imparts His holy righteous nature and eternal life to our regenerate spirit. Thus we become partakers of His divine nature, in our spirit man. This divine nature is in our new man, which after God is created in righteousness and true holiness. It is the 'seed' of God imparted to individuals in regeneration, which "cannot sin."

"By the righteousness of one, the free gift came upon all men, unto justification of life." When Jesus was "made sin", our sins were imputed to Him; set down to his account or charged to his account. Jesus sacrificial death satisfied divine justice on our behalf. By merit of the Lord's sacrifice on our behalf, we were made the righteousness of God in Christ Jesus. Jesus righteousness was imputed to us, set down to our account, freely bestowed to us as a gift, by God's amazing mercy and grace. Receiving the righteousness of God is a matter of understanding and receiving the gift of righteousness by faith. It has absolutely nothing whatsoever to do with any law of works of obedience on the believer's behalf. The just live by faith! It is a done deal! Faith is the requirement. Faith to know, and truly believe that we are indeed the righteousness of God in Christ Jesus, can only be appropriated by individuals through knowledge of God's word. Faith comes through knowledge of God's word.

It is so easy to allow ourselves to be seduced into trusting in acts of obedience, and obeying a law of works, for right standing with God. However it is a death trap which brings us under the judgment of the Law, whereby we find ourselves in a cursed situation. This sad state of affairs comes about because we are longer submitting to the righteousness which God has freely provided for us as a gift, by His amazing mercy and grace.

Unforgiveness can also cause us to lose God's blessing, whereby we find ourselves under a curse. Brother Zosimo is also a student and working member at Covenant Keepers, here in the Philippines. He came hobbling towards me the other day, in great pain in his right foot, finding it very difficult to walk, "I have arthritis, please pray for me."

"Has someone done you an injustice, and you have not forgiven them?" He nodded his head.

"Unforgiveness brings you under the curse of the law. Even if it was all their fault and you are the innocent party, you must forgive, so that God can forgive you." He took the offender to the Lord, and forgave. I prayed, and he was instantly set free from the curse. In actual fact, he jumped up and down on what had been the painful foot, and praised the Lord.

Ignorance and unbelief concerning the atonement in Christ Jesus, is also a means whereby we find ourselves in a cursed situation.

Eating the Bread and Wine in unbelief and ignorance concerning what the elements of the Covenant symbolize, also brings the judgment of the Law upon individuals, whereby they find themselves in a cursed situation.

Having other gods before the Lord, by having more trust in the remedies of the world for healing, than in the Covenant in Christ's stripes, can also cause one to come under the judgment of the Law, whereby we find ourselves in a cursed situation.

Trusting in self-effort and obedience to a law of works, also brings the judgment of the Law against individuals, whereby we find ourselves in a cursed situation, which was my own experience. When I was dying of typhoid fever God intervened and spoke the following words to me, in an audible voice. "YOU MUST GIVE THE MESSAGE TO THE CHURCH." The message is, get out from religious law keeping, and live by grace through faith in the completed work of the atonement in Christ our Lord.

Chapter Ten

I was on the move again, headed towards Laguna, to encourage two of the Lord's Filipino handmaidens, Sisters Mary and Susan who were called of God to start a Christian Fellowship in that area. En route I found myself in a jeepney with a group of young people dressed in green and white checked uniforms. They were all carrying Bibles. This I discovered was a divine appointment arranged by the Lord Himself. I began to witness to them about my trip to the mountain Provinces, and shared the miracles I had seen the Lord perform. They listened keenly until their eyes were almost standing out on stalks with amazement. Then a young man spoke, "We have been taught that the gifts of the Holy Ghost and miracles ceased when the apostles died."

"I have never heard of such a bizarre doctrine, I have been a channel through whom God has demonstrated many miracles, as I have just explained to you."

"You cannot build doctrines on experiences" then said another student.

"I am not building doctrines on my experiences. I have simply obeyed the Great Commission, opening my Bible I read it aloud."

Then a young lady blurted out, "The great commission was only for the first century saints."

"Have you preached the gospel yet?"

"Yes, we are on our way to an outreach meeting now!"

"But you should not be preaching the gospel if the Great Commission was an instruction only for the first century saints. How can you detach the preaching of the

111

gospel from the rest of the Lord's commission?"

That remark caused their eyes to open wider. "Have you been baptized the Bible way, by full immersion?"

"Yes, we have all been baptized since we believed."

"You should not have done that. You say the Great Commission was an instruction given only to the first century saints. How can you detach preaching the gospel and baptism from the remainder of Jesus commission to his body? Please give me scriptural evidence which proves your doctrine." They looked at each other and shook their heads, and could not find a scripture to verify their doctrine.

Those beautiful big brown eyes took on a questioning look, and I continued, "It is not Biblically correct to separate the preaching of the gospel and believer's baptism from the rest of the Lord's Commission, it must be fulfilled in its entirety. Before God can use you to demonstrate His miraculous power you must be endued with power, evidenced by speaking in tongues, the supernatural language of the Holy Ghost." At that point two of the girls began to cry, under conviction of God's Spirit. Leaning over the passage-way between the seats, I laid my hands on their shoulders, praying in the language of the Holy Ghost. To my amazement they immediately burst into tongues. The Spirit of God was doing a new thing in the lives of these young believers. The anointing was powerful, and some of the young men slipped off the seat and to their knees on the passage-way between the two rows of seats. They raised their hands in total submission to the Lord, and I laid my hands on them praying in tongues. One by one, they burst out speaking in tongues. God's Spirit within them was freed and released from the bondage of false doctrine. It was an amazing thing to happen in the back of a moving jeepney, in the midst of the traffic jammed streets of Manila. God never fails to amaze me, He is no respecter of people or places, and does the necessary wherever he finds willing open vessels. Endowed with Holy Ghost power, these youngsters would go on to do great and mighty things, that the Father might be glorified in His Son.

After this great event was concluded by God's Spirit, the students were full of questions. I turned to the scriptures, and let the Lord answer their queries through His own word.

Even the timing was perfect. When all their questions were satisfactorily answered, we arrived at the place where I would catch the bus for Laguna. Sisters Mary and Susan met me at the bus terminal in Laguna, and I immediately discerned that they were downcast and discouraged. As we traveled to their home in a hired jeepney, they started to tell me about the persecution they had faced. The roof of their home had been stoned on a regular basis over the months they had been there. By the power of the indwelling Holy Ghost, they stood their ground and prayed for their persecutors, even though they did not know who their persecutors were. By the time they went out side to investigate the stoning, there was not a soul to be seen.

They had no church building, so meetings were conducted in homes, and we had a small revival. Backslidden believers returned to the Lord, believers were baptized in the Holy Ghost, evidenced by speaking in tongues. The Lord worked with us confirming His word with signs following, and believers were healed of their pains, ailments and sicknesses. The two Pastors were greatly encouraged in their calling, to see the Lord work so mightily in our midst. I left them with a new zeal and determination to carry on.

My visa was due to expire and it was time to ask the Lord whether he wanted me to return to England or continue to serve Him in the Philippines. "You know my heart Lord. I only want to be where you want me to be." Events revealed that it was God's will that I returned to my native country at that particular time.

Chapter Eleven

I was home! After the tropical heat of the Philippines I found my native land very cold and shivered for the first week while I became acclimatized to British weather. I was home, but had no home to return to, and my only worldly possessions were packed in my suitcase. My future lay in the mind of God. My Lord, who had taken care of me and provided for me in the Philippines, would continue to be my guide and provider. For the present I would lodge with my friend Maria, until the Lord gave further leading and direction.

Norwich was the city from which I had gone to the Philippines, and the place to which I returned. I wanted all my friends to know what I had seen and learnt in the mountains of Northern Luzon. I wanted everyone to know that the name of our Lord Christ is the most powerful name in the universe. I wanted everyone to know that Jesus is the same yesterday, today and forever. I wanted every one to know Jesus as their Saviour, healer and provider. Bursting with enthusiasm, my mouth would not stop talking about the wonderful works I had seen God perform in the Philippines. I met a Christian couple at a wedding reception, and with my very zealous enthusiasm shared my testimony. They listened with full attention and then asked me to share my testimony with their House Fellowship in Devon. This invitation led to many more as the news spread of the great things God was doing.

The Devon people opened their hearts to me, and I was welcomed with love and practical kindness all over the South Hams. It was a time of revival in the district, and believers were built up in the faith and baptized in the Holy Ghost evidenced by speaking in tongues. Hundreds of people received their sins forgiven by responding to God's grace and accepted Jesus as their sin bearer, healer and Saviour. Many hundreds were also set free of many and varied sicknesses and ailments, so many that I cannot remember the details. Some, however, were more amazing than others and were lodged in my memory.

The following is a letter I received from farmer Herbert Rew:

"In December 1981, you came to our area and subsequently came to our house, where on occasions a number of people came to hear your testimony, and to receive healing as you prayed for them in the name of the Lord Jesus Christ. As a young man I abused my back; as one orthopedic doctor told me, I had worn out the vertebrae in my back. Consequently I was very restricted in my movements and if I was not careful then I suffered back pain for a period. I have twice spent periods encased in a plaster jacket, and have had to wear a steel brace to restrict my movements and further damage. As you prayed for me I was aware of things happening in my back, and was confident that my back was renewed. I put the brace away from that evening. Since that time I have been able to do things I have been unable to do for twenty years. One example is particularly worthy of note. Just three days after the renewal of my back, I was erecting some sheep fencing and I could see that the old iron hayrack would be ideal to stop one hole in the fence. The hayrack was heavy, certainly much too heavy for someone with a suspect back. I picked it up and placed it where it was required. No problem!

If we receive miracles in our life then we should be aware that the devil would try and challenge us. This happened to me in a very dramatic way at the beginning of

August. I was at a cattle market intending to buy some cattle when my back started to feel uncomfortable. As time went on I had real pain in my back such as I had not experienced since my healing. I moved around but the pain persisted. I finished the business I intended to do and got into my Land Rover and drove for about one mile the pain getting worse and worse to the point at which it was almost unbearable. I must confess that for a moment I began to doubt. Then I reasoned it was the devil attacking me. Then and there I said, "I command you evil spirit in the name of Jesus Christ depart from me and leave me alone". The pain stopped immediately and I have not felt it since. Praise the Lord for the power in His name."

I was often called to pray for people in their homes when they were not able to come to the meetings. One such person was named Melvina who had suffered a stroke, and was facing a bleak future imprisoned in a wheel chair and completely dependent on other people. She wrote me a brief note dated, 27th August 1982:

"On the 1st of April I had a stroke and was paralyzed down my right side. I could not move. I was told by doctors and nurses that I would never walk or cope with stairs again, and would be confined to a wheelchair for the rest of my life. You called on me and prayed and thanks be to God, three days after your visit I started to walk and I am now fully recovered. I am remembering you in my prayers."

Richard had been suffering with an ulcer for approximately eighteen months, he was a born again believer but had been taught that miracles ceased when the apostles died, so his only help was the medical profession. The treatment he was receiving had to be suspended because he had developed an allergic reaction to his medication. His doctor was waiting for the drug rash to subside before starting him on a new course of treatment.

He wrote from his home in Salcombe:

"While the rash was going down, everything I ate seemed like red hot gravel going into my stomach (which according to my wife makes a man very bad tempered). I heard about a meeting to be held in Kingsbridge by Isabel Chapman. Studying the scriptures again I could find no foundation for the teaching that miracles ended with the death of the apostles, so I determined to go along and decide for myself. With many others that night I went forward to be prayed for. You asked me what I required from the Lord. I had been feeling my lack of power as a lay preacher and I asked that I might have the power of the Holy Spirit in my preaching and that the ulcer be healed. You asked if I spoke in tongues and I replied that I did not. You asked if I wanted the gift of tongues and I said, "Not particularly" At this time you asked the Lord to heal me, prayed in a language I could not understand, and thanked the Lord for healing me. Your parting words were, "Exercise your faith, brother!"

Off I went to exercise my faith, which I did for a week and nothing happened. The pain was as bad as ever. So I went to the next meeting, which you held in Marlborough and you prayed for me again. Next morning my breakfast went down perfectly; there was no pain. For the past six months I have had a new awareness of God's love and power. Our Father God, Son and Holy Spirit, are the same as in the days of the Apostles."

In the Philippines we always baptized new converts the Bible way by full immersion according to the instructions of God's word.

He that believeth and is baptized shall be saved;

But he that believeth not shall be dammed. Mark 16:15.

The majority of the believers in the South Hams were baptized as infants, but I reasoned with them that the Bible taught that repentance must come before baptism, that baptism was an act of obedience after one has been born of God's Spirit. An infant cannot repent, as it has no knowledge of sin. I did not realize that I was walking into an ecclesiastical mine field, and that the religious leaders were up in arms against me, and accusing me of leading people astray. My response was that Jesus had called me to walk in obedience to His word. Therefore I was not willing to compromise with man-made religious traditions.

Through a word of prophecy I received in 1980, the Lord forewarned me that I would be opposed by the religious leaders of my day, even as He and His disciples were in their day.

"I have called you, my daughter. Part of your work is this: you will be a repairer of the breach, though at the moment you do not understand what the breach is. The breach is in the Kingdom of God. I have picked you, and will use you to show my glory in the earth, regardless of men and religiosity. You shall stand and you shall be open, and I shall reveal my purposes to you. You will not only know me as Christ, but you will know me as a deliverer and as the Father of Israel before all is done. You will know me as a son, and as a bride knows her husband. You will know me as the God of the universe; for I have shown you but an inkling, yes, only a jot and tittle of what my wonders can perform. I have picked you and lifted you up because of your obedience and because of your heart. I have set you in a realm of victory. My word shall find a stable place in your heart wherever you go. You may feel as Jeremiah when he said, Lord, I am only a youth; they will not listen to me. But I tell you that Israel had hardened her heart at that time and would not listen to the truth of her deliverance. As for you, I shall take you and I shall confound the men who set themselves as the scribes and Pharisee and Sadducees of this day. I shall show the revelation of Jesus Christ in you, and you shall be used in this day. For there are those whose hearts have been hardened by the education they have

received, because of the ways of the world that have been taught them, and they have closed their hearts to the truth.

But I shall take delight in you my daughter, because of the simplicity of my word in your heart, because of the truth that is within you. You will perform my works, and you will see the Lord of Hosts revealed, not only in yourself, but in your dwelling place, in your circumstances, and wherever you go. Hearken to my word, it shall not only set you free, but it shall set others free also. You will stand amazed at what God will perform through you. You are appointed and anointed by me, a special vessel unto me. Fear not my daughter, though people rise up against you. Every tongue that speaks against you will be condemned by you, for this is the prerogative of the saints. I have called you in due time, for these are the end-days and you will be faithful. My glory will be revealed in an even greater realm, and as you see these things, you will understand that you are truly a son. Because I have declared that my Kingdom will be established forever and ever. For I will bring you into a blessing and dimension that you have not yet known. You shall see mighty miracles, and multitudes will come unto God. Because you have been faithful to my word, it shall not return unto me void. You shall go forth mighty to do and mighty to conquer because you go in my name, says the Lord your God who loves you."

Regardless of opposition I arranged a Baptismal service in Paignton Bay. We fixed an afternoon at a time when everyone could come, and prayed for fine weather. The day arrived but it was a cold, wet, rainy morning, so I reached out in prayer to the Lord, asking Him to move the rain clouds away from Paignton Bay. By the time we arrived at the beach, the morning rain had rolled away, and the biggest and brightest rainbow I had ever seen greeted us. It spanned the entire bay in a gigantic arc. Our Covenant keeping God revealed His presence, and confirmed His approval of this special baptismal ceremony. How it thrilled my heart that the Lord was revealing His presence and approval to the baptismal candidates, who had been rebuked by their ministers for being re-baptized. Our Covenant Keeping God was smiling down at His children as they disregarded religious tradition to obey His word - believe and be baptized. Our oldest candidate stepped into the freezing cold waters, at the great age of over eighty years, and was baptized in the name of the Father and of the Son and of the Holy Ghost. It was a memorable event, which brought my ministry in the South Hams to a conclusion. The Lord was moving me on.

Chapter Twelve

I had a long-standing invitation from Hamish Cormach to visit Wick in the Highlands of Scotland. By the time I arrived there I had traversed the entire length of England and Scotland. On that long journey stretching the length of the British Isles, the Holy Ghost spoke to my spirit concerning the forth-coming ministry:

Many hearts lie dormant, many hearts long to be aflame in my service. Call forth that flame, cause it to burn in my service. Help my people to know who they are in me, so that miracles may be performed for my Glory. Then hands, which are stretched forth in love, shall know my healing power. Show the grace and power of my providence in your life, despite your smallness and frailty.

Brother Hamish was a Church of Scotland minister who had done an excellent job of advertising the meetings, so unbelievers attended the church meetings as well as eager believing members of Christ's Body. God wanted to use me as a channel to give His people understanding of who they are 'in' Christ Jesus. First they had to understand that we are the righteousness of God 'in' Christ Jesus. We have no righteousness of our own that we can offer to Jesus, as we have all sinned and fallen short of the glory of God. The bride of Christ is a glorious church, not having spot, or wrinkle, or any such thing, and is holy and without blemish.

Ephesians 5 v 27

That he might present to himself a glorious church, not having spot, or wrinkle, or any such thing; but that it should be holy and without blemish.

The appearing of Jesus in the air to "catch up" His holy

bride was burning in my heart. I believe we are living in the last days of this dispensation of amazing grace. These are the day's preparation. The Bridegroom is preparing to go out to meet His bride. The bride is being fitted with her wedding garment of fine linen clean and white, having neither spot nor wrinkle, or any such thing. The wedding garment has been especially chosen and provided by the King, for His elect bride. The bride who will attend the greatest wedding banquet of all time cannot choose her own wedding garment. She must be adorned with the wedding garment which has been especially chosen and freely provided by the amazing grace of the Father and the Son, and is revealed by the Holy Ghost, through God's word. The true church, and bride of Christ, must be clothed in a wedding garment that glorifies and magnifies the grace of the Holy Trinity. The bride's wedding garment is the righteousness of the elect chosen saints, Christ's righteousness imputed to us, which we wear as a garment by faith. Our wedding garment is the gift of God's amazing grace, freely provided for us through the death and redeeming blood of Jesus Christ, the Saviour of sinners. Christ's righteousness, worn as a garment by faith, presents us holy and blameless before the great judge who sits on the Throne of Glory. He who has called us out of darkness into his marvelous light has declared: (1 Peter 1: 6)

"Be ye holy for I am holy!"

The only righteousness that God accepts is perfect righteousness – the righteousness of the Lord Jesus Christ, by which Jesus fulfilled the Law on our behalf. According to the Lord's leading to me, the congregation at Wick had to be made to understand that there are two kinds of righteousness at work in this world, self-righteousness and Christ's imputed righteousness, and that the Lord God Almighty only accepts perfect righteousness. The only righteousness which is perfect righteousness is the righteousness of Jesus Christ. From birth to death Jesus perfectly kept the Ten Commandments and never committed a single sin. To be holy, as our God is holy, we must be clothed, by faith, in the robe of righteousness which Jesus' Holy redeeming blood freely provided for His bride. The wedding garment is the righteousness of the saints, not our self-righteous performance, but Christ's righteousness.

To get this vital point over to the congregation, I walked down the aisle and asked individuals the question. "Have you sinned since you were born again?" All, without exception, had to confess that they had sinned since they were saved, which agrees with Romans 3:10 – "There is none righteous, no, not one."

"We fallen mortal beings have no righteousness of our own that we can offer to our holy God, and God refuses to accept self-righteousness wrought by personal performance, good works and abstinence. The only righteousness that God accepts is Christ's perfect righteousness, which is imputed to the believer by God's amazing grace and received by individuals by faith, through knowledge of the promises in God's word. Christ's Imputed righteousness worn as a garment by faith is our wedding garment and our passport home to the Eternal City, where we will attend the wedding feast of the Lamb.

"The consequences of sin in the Garden of Eden brought shame and fear upon Adam and Eve - this is revealed by the fact that they ran and hid from God's presence. The eyes of their conscience were opened, and they saw that they were naked – no longer dressed in the righteousness garment which God had provided for them. God created Adam in His own image and likeness, perfectly holy and righteous, possessing eternal life. Adam's eyes were opened, his sin was exposed, and he saw that they had lost the image and likeness of the Creator. Adam had fallen from the state of being pure, holy and blameless, sin caused the Holy Ghost to depart from him, and thus he lost the gift of eternal life, and was cut of from union with God.

"This is the reason we must be born again. We were all born into this world bearing Adam's hereditary sin nature, cut off from union with God, and separated from the life of God. When individuals accept Jesus' death and blood as full ransom payment for all their sins, and believe that Jesus rose from death, the Holy Ghost comes and takes up residence within us, and we are joined to God, united with God – born of the seed of God. The indwelling Holy Ghost imparts the image and likeness and eternal life of Jesus to our spirit, in the miracle of rebirth. Thus we are created a new creation in Christ Jesus. The image and likeness of God is lodged in our spirit man, therefore we experience the reverse of what happened to Adam.

"Adam and Eve tried to make amends and cover over their sinful state by making a covering for themselves but God could not accept these human "works" in place of His perfect covering. Also Divine Justice declares, *"The wages of sin is death", and "without the shedding of blood there is no remission for sin."* The only acceptable payment for sin is death and sacrificial blood. Divine Justice had to be satisfied. The Lord God warned them, "If you eat from the forbidden tree you will surely die!" And they did die, and Adam's sin put all humanity under the death penalty of physical death to be followed by the second death – eternal damnation.

"Almighty God had known that Adam would use his free will to rebel against His will. Our all-knowing Father had already made provision for the fall, and set in motion His perfect plan of Salvation. God the Father made a

Covenant agreement with our first parents, whereby animals were put to death as their substitute. The death and blood of the innocent sacrifices appeased Divine Justice. Therefore God and sinner were reconciled. God then clothed Adam and Eve with *coats of skins* taken from the animals that were put to death and bled as their substitute sin offering. The *coats of skins* were a *righteous garment,* freely provided by God's amazing grace, through the atoning death and blood of substitute sacrifices.

"The righteous garment had to be received by *faith,* through belief that the death and blood of their sin offering had satisfied Divine Justice on their behalf. Their righteous garment worn by faith provided them with right standing in the presence of their Holy God, and saved them from the second death, eternal damnation. The *coats of skins* were their robes of righteousness, which God freely provided for them by His amazing grace.

Our heavenly Father, the Almighty God, is good all the time, full of love, mercy, amazing grace and unconditional agape love towards sinners, therefore He did not damn our first parents because of their transgressions. On the contrary, He made a way of escape for them.

"Throughout Old Covenant times, God's chosen people the Jews sacrificed animals as a sin offering, the animals died as the sinners' substitutes. Atonement for sin through the death and blood of substitute sacrificial animals took place yearly on the Day of Atonement. The death of the substitution animals satisfied divine justice on the sinner's behalf. The sacrificial animals were bled, and the blood was carried by the high priest into the Holy of Holies, and sprinkled on the mercy seat to atone for sins committed. The sacrificial blood 'covered' the sins of God's chosen people and provided them a garment of righteousness, which kept them in right standing with their

Holy God.

"The sacrificing of animals on the Day of Atonement was a schoolmaster to teach fallen humanity why God in Christ would come into our world and give His sinless Holy body and blood, as the once for all perfect sacrifice for sin. Some people see God only as the God of judgment, waiting for the first opportunity to send sinners to damnation. This however, is a completely wrong concept. God is good all the time and full of love, mercy, grace compassion and unconditional love for the His fallen human race.

"God refused to accept Adam and Eve's attempt to cover their sinful state with a garment made from fig leaves because they could not save themselves by self-effort. The death and blood of a substitute was the only accepted ransom payment for sin, according to Divine law. Divine Justice required a Holy, sinless blood sacrifice to pay the full penalty for sin and set humanity free from the consequences of sin, and in the fullness of time God planned to make a body for Himself in a virgin's womb. In this manner, He would come from heaven to earth, the purpose of His earthly mission to give His own sinless life as the *once for all*, perfect sacrifice for sin. By His own death and Holy redeeming blood He would buy humanity back to Himself, and free us from sin's power to curse us with the curse of the Law, which includes the curse of eternal separation from God – suffering in the Lake of fire and brimstone – eternal damnation.

"The Lord Jesus Christ was the promised Messiah, Emmanuel, God come to earth in a human body. (Col 2:9) God used the sacrificing of animals as practiced by the Jews during the days of the Old Covenant, to teach fallen humanity that the day would come when the Promised Messiah would fulfill the animal type, by laying down his own life as the sacrificial Lamb of God, to take away the sins of the world.

"Sinful fallen humanity cannot be saved by self-righteous living, good works or abstinence. The death and Holy blood of a sinless sacrifice is the required payment, which was paid in full, by the sacrificial death and Holy redeeming blood of the God-Man, our Saviour, our Redeemer, our Sacrificial Lamb and Sin Bearer, our Lord Jesus Christ. The death and blood of sacrificial animals 'covered sin.' The death and holy redeeming blood of Jesus 'cancelled out' the sins of the world, from Adam's day till the end of this present dispensation. The price of sin is fully paid; sin is no longer separating us from God. God is no longer imputing sin to believers; He is not keeping a record of our sins. Sin is no longer the issue, the issue now is "Do you accept Christ Jesus as your Saviour and sin bearer? Do you believe that Christ's death and blood was the accepted perfect sacrifice and ransom payment for the sins of fallen humanity? Can you accept your sins forgiven and cancelled on your behalf, annulled, through faith in the atonement in Christ's death and holy redeeming blood?"

The congregation was busy with handkerchiefs, wiping tears from their eyes. One man stood up with hands raised toward heaven and cried, "Thank you Jesus, I accept you as my sin bearer and Saviour. I thought I would never make the grade. I thought I would never be good enough to be a Christian. Now I understand that salvation was freely accomplished for me, by your amazing grace, through Christ's death and blood." The Holy Ghost took up residence within him, regenerated his spirit and endowed him with power. Words in a heavenly language poured from his mouth as if a dam had burst.

Many in the congregation were set free from a false gospel of 'works', to understanding that we are saved by grace through faith, in the finished work of the atonement in Christ Jesus, and not of by self-effort or keeping a religious law of works. Salvation is the gift of God, not of works lest any man boast. (Eph 2:8-10) The congregation was greatly relieved to understand that they were not responsible for trying to save them selves by good living standards and works of self-righteousness. Truth is, self-righteousness breeds pride, which is contrary to the humble spirit of our Lord.

Wick was now experiencing revival. The match had been struck, the flame was beginning to burn in the hearts of the people. Even in small town meetings there were many sick people who needed prayer, old and young alike, and God worked with me, confirming His word with signs following.

On the second evening I continued with the theme of the Lord's appearing in the *AIR*, to "catch up" living believers as recorded in 1Thes 4:16-18.

"The final resurrection of the "dead in Christ" will take place when Jesus appears in the air in resurrection power. The dead in Christ will rise first. The bodies of the dead saints will be miraculously resurrected in immortality, and united with their spirit and soul, which went directly home to be with the Lord as they passed through the valley of the shadow of death. Living believers on earth will be "caught up" to meet the Lord in the air. The living mortal body will be miraculously changed; the mortal will put on immortality. This will happen in an atom of time, by the miraculous resurrection power of our Lord Jesus Christ. The same mighty miraculous power that raised Jesus from death will resurrect the bodies of the dead saints, which have been reduced to dust, and will miraculously and supernaturally change our mortal bodies, into immortal bodies, and translate us from earth to meet Jesus in the air.

So shall we ever be with the Lord. Comfort one another with these words.

Such an amazing, supernatural, miraculous event may be difficult to comprehend. We cannot comprehend it, God's miraculous supernatural power is beyond human carnal understanding. All we have to do is simply believe God's word, and receive by faith that this will actually happen to us. God is not a man that He can lie. Dismiss your doubts, as the devil is the liar.

I have no problem believing that my mortal body will be miraculously changed into an immortal body, nor do I have any unbelief concerning being instantaneously, miraculously translated from earth to heaven. I have already experienced being instantly and miraculously translated from one place to another by the supernatural power of Almighty God. It happened in America during a short ministry tour. I was traveling with a sister who was a medical doctor. During the evening meeting the night before, the Lord instantly and miraculously had healed a broken bone in her left arm, and she was full of awe, joy and gratitude for her miracle. We were on our way to a convention, and were following Pastor Dorn and his family. I had been at the wheel for hours keeping the Dorn's bronze colored car in view, as our guiding pigeon leading the way because neither of us had any local knowledge of where this convention was to be held. Suddenly we realized that we had lost our pigeon, the Dorn's car was nowhere to be seen. Stepping on the accelerator, I sped along the highway in an attempt to catch up with the bronze colored car.

We had to face the fact that they must have turned off the highway without our seeing them and our hearts sank. We were lost, what should we do? Prayer was the only answer. I pulled into the side of the road and prayed a simple but heartfelt prayer. We were two lost handmaids who needed our Fathers intervention. "Heavenly Father, we are lost, please *somehow* get us back behind the Dorns' car, this we ask in Jesus name." Holding on to the steering wheel with eyes closed and bowed head, I began to pray in the Holy Ghost, and my companion followed suit. When I opened my eyes I was driving along the highway and our bronze pigeon was right in front of us. There is only one explanation, the prayer of faith moved God to move on our behalf, the mighty hand of our Heavenly Father supernaturally intervened and translated us in an atom of time, back behind our traveling companions.

Arriving at our destination and climbing stiffly out of our vehicles after the long drive, Pastor Dorn came up to us and said. "What happened to you two? You disappeared for quite some time, we did not know what to do, but decided to keep going and trust the Lord that all was well. Then you appeared out of the blue, one moment I looked in the rear mirror and there was no sight of you, the next moment I looked, there you were – very strange!" We shared our testimony of what had happened, and he remarked, "Nothing is impossible with God when you are around, Isabel!" He should have said, "Nothing is impossible with God, when we pray the prayer of faith."

"The point I am making is that God watches over His word to perform it, He has promised to translate us from earth to glory in an atom of time, and change our mortal bodies for immortal bodies, by His own mighty miraculous power. The day is coming when it will happen, to all who believe the testimony of His word. Mortality belongs to this present world. Immortality belongs to the Eternal world. First we have a mortal body, and then we have an immortal body. As we have born the image of Adam's natural mortal body, so shall we also bear the image of our Redeemer's resurrected, glorified immortal body. The raising of the dead in immortality, and the 'catching up' and 'change' of the body, from being in a mortal state, to possessing a glorified immortal body, will happen as quickly as it takes to blink the eye. We see a picture of what we have yet to experience in Revelation 7: 9 -10. This is a foretaste or picture of the New Covenant saints praising God in our glorified immortal bodies, in the Eternal City, Jerusalem above.

After this I beheld, and lo, a great multitude, which no man could number, of all nations, and kindreds, and people, and tongues, stood before the throne, and before the lamb, clothed with white robes, and palms in their hands; and cried with a loud voice, saying, SALVATION TO OUR GOD WHICH SITTETH UPON THE THRONE, AND UNTO THE LAMB. Rev 7:10.

"This is indeed a vision that thrills the heart and spirit of all believers. Multitudes of blood-bought believers out of every nation on the face of the earth, standing before the throne of God in the Eternal City, with Jesus our Passover Lamb. Through the eye of faith we can see our loved ones who have passed through the valley of the shadow of death, clothed in immortality. We see death swallowed up in victory. We also see ourselves clothed in immortality, wearing white robes, our wedding garment. Our redemption will then be complete, we will be clothed in immortality and forever separated from sin and the consequences of sin, there will be no more crying, no more pain, no more sorrow and no more death. We shall eternally abide with our God and go on to discover the wonders and glories of what our Lord has prepared for us through out eternity.

Revelation 19: 7-9

Let us be glad and rejoice, and give honour to him: for

the marriage of the lamb has come, and his wife hath made herself ready. And to her was granted that she should be arrayed in fine linen, clean and white: for the fine linen is the righteousness of the saints. And he said unto me, Write, Blessed are they, which are called unto the marriage supper of the lamb. And he said unto me, these are the true sayings of God.

"Even at earthly weddings, the guests are expected to appear wearing an acceptable garment, fitted for the great occasion. How much more, should we appear wearing the acceptable garment, fitted for the greatest wedding ever, the uniting of Jesus with His bride? Then our redemption will be completed and perfected. We cannot buy our wedding garment, no amount of silver, gold, diamonds, or self-righteous living can purchase our wedding garment. Our Bridegroom has freely granted or freely bestowed the wedding garment to His bride. He purchased it for us, with the great price of His own death and atoning holy blood. Our wedding garment is received by faith in the accomplishment of the sacrificial death and atoning blood of Christ our Redeeming Saviour. He (Jesus) was made to be sin for us, that is, a sin offering, that we be made the righteousness of God in Christ Jesus. (2 Corinthians 5:21)

"Our wedding garment of fine linen clean and white, is Christ's imputed righteousness, which He has freely granted to all, by His amazing grace. The wedding garment can only be received by grace through faith, in the atonement in Christ's sacrificial death and holy redeeming blood. Our wedding garment is *faith righteousness*. Without faith it is impossible to please God. We see a picture of a self-righteous believer who tried to attend the great wedding banquet by his own merit, in Mathew 22:11-14.

When the king came in to see the guests, he saw there a man which had not on a wedding garment: And he said unto him, Friend, how camest thou in hither not having a wedding garment? And he was speechless. Then said the king to the servants, Bind him hand and foot, and take him away, and cast him into outer darkness; there shall be weeping and gnashing of teeth. For many are called but few are chosen.

"Imagine the scene. Multitudes of believers in the banquet hall dressed in white robes, waving palms as a mark of honor, gratitude, praise, worship, adoration and love for Jesus, who washed us clean in His own holy redeeming blood. With bated breath, we await the moment we have longed for all our lives, to see our Redeemer face to face. The Lamb of God appears in all his glory, and makes the grand entrance as "King of Kings and Lord of Lords." We fall on our faces before His Majesty and Glory, and begin to worship Him, who redeemed us from damnation with His own death and blood. Suddenly, the King raises his hand and points to someone in the midst of the great multitude and calls out. "Friend, how did you get in here not having a wedding garment?" The accused stood before the King, naked, as naked as was Adam after the fall. His sin was exposed for all to see. He did not have a case, and was unable to utter a word in self defence, he was speechless, dumbfounded.

"The man was clothed in a garment of self-righteousness, which denied the full sufficiency of the sacrificial death and Holy atoning blood of the King of Kings and Lord of Lords. The devil had deceived this man into believing that his particular religious denomination was the only true church of God. He strictly obeyed his spiritual leaders who wore long religious robes. He regularly attended church, and had given up all vices and bad habits, by his determination and will power. He was a good self-righteous man, the pillar of society type. But the

King would not accept the sinner's own attempt to be holy. The required payment for sin was the death and blood of the King of Kings and Lord of Lords – the very death of God Almighty. "Bind him hand and foot, and take him away, and cast him into outer darkness; there shall be weeping and gnashing of teeth.

"There is a day coming, when all who trust in self-righteous law keeping and abstinence, for right standing with God, will face the same end as this self-righteous religious sinner. Weeping and wailing and gnashing of teeth, is a description of torment in the lake of fire and brimstone. It is an expression of frustration, pain, torment, rage, anger, bitterness, hatred, resentment, indignation and fury against Christ and his power to condemn them and their master Satan, to eternal damnation.

Many are called but few are chosen! It is not God's will that any perish in that terrible place called the lake of fire and brimstone. God does not choose some to be dammed and others to be saved. God is no respecter of persons, and He has made a way for all sinners to be saved through Jesus Christ, who is the only way to the Father. The chosen ones choose to be chosen, by taking time out to get to know God through the scriptures, and by accepting God's word as truth. We choose to be chosen, by responding to God's amazing grace and accepting Christ Jesus as our Saviour and sin bearer. Those who reject Christ's sacrificial death as payment for their sin must pay the penalty for their own sins. The penalty is eternal torment, the second death.

"Not only has Jesus paid the full penalty for your sins, and cancelled out your sin record once for all time. He has removed the consequences of sin, which is the curse of the Law - sickness, pain, suffering and poverty as well as the second death."

In conclusion, I said to the assembled company, "If you

have received your forgiveness by faith, come and receive your healing by faith." Nearly the entire congregation left their seats and came forward for prayer. They were all under the judgment of the law, because the majority were trusting in obedience to a law of works, good living standards and abstinence for right standing with God. Those who live by Law must perfectly keep the Law, and no one is capable of perfectly keeping the Law. They were all under the curse of the Law.

Facing the congregation I read Galatians 3: 13.

"Christ has redeemed you from the curse of the Law-sickness, pain, disease and the second death. To walk in the blessings you must live by grace, through faith in the perfect atonement in Christ Jesus. Stop trying to please God and gain His favour by your efforts and religious law keeping. Only faith in the atonement in the Lord's death and blood, can cancel your sin record, and clothe you with an acceptable righteous garment. Cast off your self-righteous garments of fig leaves, and clothe yourselves by faith, in Christ's imputed righteousness, and the curse will instantly leave you. Believe that Jesus bore your sicknesses and carried your pains, when He bore the agony of the scourge as your scape goat. Receive your healing now, according to the word of the Lord. Christ has redeemed you from the curse of the law."

I moved amongst the people, praying in tongues and laying hands on them. They were set free from the curse, and the healing power of the Lord was flowing like a river. People began to testify of being healed of all kinds of ailments and diseases. Truly, Christ has redeemed us from the curse of the Law.

Chapter Thirteen

My hostess at Wick was dear Miss Emma Bruce, a retired music teacher and loving saint of God. Her letter to me included the following testimony:

"Only yesterday, a young woman stopped me in the street with a little girl of four, an adopted child who had been profoundly deaf. She was healed instantly when you prayed for her and now they are spreading the Good News and rejoicing in the Lord."

I remembered addressing the spirit of deafness, and commanding it to loose its hold on the child, in the name of the Lord Jesus Christ. Instantly she put her hands to her ears as if to block out the noise. I knew she had been set free, but it was good to read the testimony from Emma.

Roderick, a twelve-year-old boy, who was prone to urinary infections throughout his childhood, had been medically diagnosed as having a congenital obstruction of his urinary tract. Roderick wrote the following testimony:

"A woman evangelist came to our church in Wick. Her sermons were amazing and gave me knowledge of what was going to happen to those who do not know God, and to Christians, when the end times are here. It makes me so glad to be a Christian. I always read in the Bible how God heals. I thought it was only when Jesus was on earth that people were healed, but this woman said that God still heals today. Now I happen to have had a series of operations, and I was due to go for another in five days time. I trusted that God would heal me if Isabel prayed for me, and I accepted that, by Jesus' stripes, I was healed. So, I went out and she prayed for me, and the devil had to leave me. I praise God that I never went for the operation and never will. Any time I am attacked by disease, I rebuke the devil and he has to flee."

This young lad of twelve years of age listened intently as I preached God's word, took it all most seriously, stood on the word by faith, became a doer of the word, and walked in the victory. Praise the Lord!

I did notice that the children were most attentive in the meetings in Wick. A young girl who sat near Roderick did not look well, and she looked weak, frail, pale and sickly and was like a little bird with its beak wide open, eating my every word. I remember her coming up for prayer, and was delighted to receive the following letter from her mother, Elizabeth Yaudie.

"Thought I'd give you an outline of the problem Clare has. She is nine years old. A large lump came up on the left side of her neck in the lymph gland when she was 3 years of age. Despite many different antibiotics (13 bottles of the stuff in fact) the lump was resistant to them all. A surgeon opened the lump twice and it eventually drained over several months. Needless to say she was a very ill little girl. Over this period of time she had very little energy and had to be carried about.

For the following 2-4 years she was never completely well, complaining of headaches and stomach pains. This became very acute again and all her lymphatic system became active. She would lie and weep and scream as the lymph glands swelled up all over her body. The headaches and stomach pains were diagnosed as abdominal migraine and she averaged 3-4 attacks per week, lasting anything from a couple of hours to a complete day. She was prescribed tablets (Sanomigram), which she would have to take 3 times a day, probably for life. The side effects gave her mood changes, kidney and liver damage. She changed from being a gentle loving girl into an unhappy, irritable stranger.

It was obvious that she had become allergic to many foods, probably caused by intestinal damage due to the high dosage of antibiotics over a prolonged period.

About 15-20 minutes after having food with wheat, sugar, milk, eggs or certain flavourings and colourings, Clare would be flat out on the sofa, screaming with pain. Her lymph glands in her neck would swell up so much that she seemed to have had no jawbone line.

When we came home from the meeting in Wick in December 1984, Clare said, "Mum is it true, Isabel said I could eat anything I want?" Mustering all my faith I said, "Yes, you can."

"In that case I will have a huge plate of ice cream!"

She had been unable to eat ice cream for over a year as it had the worst reaction on her, along with chocolate.

Clare sat down and ate a soup bowl of ice cream, licked her lips and duly went to bed. Over the following days, in spite of the fact that it was December and the weather was cold, she had a diet of several bowls of ice cream, and all the junk food one could imagine, and she was not ill. She eats everything and has no adverse reactions. She is on no medication of any kind. For so long we wondered if Clare was going to live, let alone live a normal life. Praise the Lord and bless you Isabel, she lives, she lives in and through our Lord Jesus Christ."

I began to get a lot of opposition from religious leaders, who told me that I was leading 'their' sheep astray, and giving them false hope of healing. They also rose up in arms against me, because I was a 'woman' preacher. They quoted the scriptures in Corinthians and Timothy. "But I suffer not a woman to teach, nor to usurp authority over the man, but to be in silence."

This really bothered me for quite some time, as I did not want to go against God's word, yet at the same time, I could not deny God's call on my life. Then I received a book from a stranger at the end of a meeting. The book set me free to be who I am in Christ Jesus. The book is entitled, "God's Word to Women" by Katherine C. Bushnell. I highly recommend this book to every woman called of God. Katherine's teaching from the original Greek and Hebrew translations set me free. It will also set you free. Follow the leading of the Holy Ghost, and be the minister of reconciliation that God has ordained you to be, regardless of religious opposition. For further details log on to gwto@godswordtowomen.org You will be blessed and encouraged.

Chapter Fourteen

After an itinerant ministry of travelling the length and breadth of my native country over a period of three years, it was God's will that I returned to the Philippines. This time I was to be met at the airport in Manila by a dear sister in Christ, Susan. Her face lit up when she saw me and we greeted each other in a loving embrace. Soon we were in the thick of the congested city traffic, which moved in fits and starts, pouring out exhaust fumes into the hot humid air. I was back in the Orient, a new adventure lay ahead. We were headed for Susan's home where I would stay the night before travelling north.

As my head hit the pillow I gave thanks to the Lord for a safe journey, and became aware of the oppressive heat and humidity, so different to the British climate and crisp cool air. It would take time to adjust, but for now I was so exhausted and nothing, or so I thought, could keep me awake. From somewhere close to the bed I could hear a continuous scratching sound.

"What's that noise, Susan?" I whispered.

"It's nothing, only rats," was the sleepy reply.

Pulling the sheet over my head, I tried to shut out the sounds of scratching rats. Now I could hear the squeaks of baby rats. Plop! A soft weight dropped from the rafters onto my bed, and scrambled across my legs. I sprang up standing on my tiptoes and pressed my body against the wall, not daring to step off the bed. Susan's voice came through the darkness. "Don't worry Isabel, they will not harm you!"

Lying back down again I spoke to the rats, "Rats, I forbid you to come onto my bed again, in the name of Jesus

Christ." They were Filipino rats who probably could not understand English, but as far as I was concerned it was accomplished in the name of my Shepherd. Even rats of whatever nationality have to obey the name above all names.

Very early the following morning, the sound of traffic from the nearby main streets penetrated my sleep and dragged me into reluctant wakefulness. By the time I had washed and dressed my clothes were already clinging to my body, from the slight exertion of getting dressed. I was definitely back in the Philippines. Within days I was in Baguio working with Pastor Padua and his wife, and we were headed for a place called Santo Thomas travelling in the normal Filipino style by jeepney.

Suddenly the jeepney came to a standstill, and everyone piled out, so I followed suit. Standing on top of a cliff, Pastor Padua pointed to a steep track that wound its way through the trees and rocks below. "There is no road into the village. We have to walk from here."

It was easy compared to walks I had done on my previous visit. There were a few believers living in this particular village who had been evangelized by the Pastor himself. Among them was an old lady, in whose home the meeting would take place later that evening. We were greeted with the usual warm friendly hospitality of the Filipino people, and a meal was prepared and waiting for us.

By the time we had finished the meal the inhabitants of the village, who had come to hear what the white woman had to say, surrounded us. Pastor Padua was my interpreter and we simply spoke of Jesus' love for them and preached the gospel of grace, which God confirmed with signs following. The first man I prayed for was in a lot of pain in his abdomen, and the Pastor told me that he had suffered with an ulcer for many years. Praying in the usual manner,

I loosed him of the spirit of infirmity in the name of the Lord Jesus Christ, emphasizing that Christ had redeemed him from the curse of the law. The pain instantly left him.

A young girl with a racking, hacking cough, was brought for prayer. I had never heard such a cough before. She was suffering under the curse of tuberculosis. She later testified, "As I was being prayed for by the missionary, I felt a cool breath of air passing through my lungs, and I do not cough any more."

These were amongst many who testified of their healing at the end of the meeting. The hike back up the rocky pathway was a hazardous undertaking in the dark. We climbed in single file following the light of the leader's torch. By the grace of God we all made it safely back to the road. Our great disappointment was that our driver and jeepney had disappeared, he probably got fed up waiting for us and decided to go home. We were approximately one hour's drive from Cruz La Trinidad where we would spend the night. My heart dropped to the bottom of my feet. It was going to be a long walk home.

We dejectedly headed up the road, and I began to pray in the Holy Ghost for strength to carry on. Then the Holy Ghost spoke to my spirit, "You have not, because you ask not!"

"Pastor, let us stop and pray the prayer of faith and agreement, and ask the Lord to send us transport."

We held hands and prayed the prayer of faith, then continued walking. Some thirty minutes later the sound of an approaching vehicle had us all running to the middle of the road and shouting, "Hallelujah." The driver had to either stop or run over us. He was not too pleased at being made to bring his vehicle to a halt in such a forced manner. Even our glowing accounts of the miracles we had just witnessed did not move him. By the time we reached our destination, we gratefully thanked him for saving us hours of walking, and a big beaming smile lit up his face. The Holy Ghost had touched his heart.

The following evening we were back in Santo Thomas. This time our driver promised to return for us, and apologized for leaving us stranded. The most memorable miracle that evening happened to a young girl. Children simply believe what they are told. With the help of my interpreter I told her, "You will be healed when I pray for you." Those big beautiful brown eyes looked into my eyes, and she nodded her head in agreement.

The child had a cancerous tumor on her left arm. She was in constant pain and could not move the arm. Her parents were very poor and could not afford to pay for hospital treatment. Thank God, Jesus makes no charge. His gift of healing is free, the only requirement is faith.

I addressed the evil spirits of death and cancer, tied them up in spiritual chains, rendered them powerless and commanded them to loose their hold of the child in the name of Jesus Christ of Nazareth. I then prayed in the power of the Holy Ghost, which released the miraculous healing power of Jesus' stripes to work in her arm. Without prompting from anyone she started to move her arm, and then she was waving it about in the air. She spoke to me but I did not understand, and Pastor Padua said, "She said, no more pain."

I took her in my arms and hugged her, and her two little arms went around my neck. Looking up, I saw her mother wiping tears from her eyes. Through those tears I saw joy and relief, and I had a fresh revelation of God's love for His suffering creation, and His great desire for people to understand, that Jesus sufferings and death had redeemed us from the curse of the Law. It was as if I heard God cry out, "My people perish through lack of knowledge."

When Jacob, our driver heard that the Pastor was planning an outreach meeting to Longlong, he threw up his arms in exasperation and exclaimed, "The road into that area is very steep and dangerous. The surface has been washed away with the heavy rains of the past rainy season. There are great potholes and boulders littering the way. My jeep is likely to get baldly damaged."

With gentle loving persuasion he agreed to give it a try, however this time we would be so far from home base that Jacob would have to stick with the team. Jacob was a religious believer who lacked the indwelling Holy Ghost, so we took it upon ourselves to pray that he would see the truth, as he sat under the preaching of God's word.

We soon found ourselves going along a road that was merely a dirt track, and I began to see why Jacob had thrown his arms in the air in exasperation at the thought of the trip. The dirt track to our destination was a continuous series of potholes. Frequently a wheel would descend into a deep cavity with a sickening thud, often wrenching the steering wheel out of our driver's control. It was a rough ride for the jeepney, and we prayed and trusted that the jeep would make it without being damaged.

At the same time we were concerned with the effect on our anatomy. Every pothole produced a boneshaking shock, and we clung to the frame to keep ourselves from being flung about. We were going up a mountain track with a cliff on one side and a ravine on the other. At one point we came to a trench the width of the road. Jacob refused to drive into it. He was hot and bothered and getting angry, but the Pastor came up with the usual Filipino remedy. Collect stones and fill in the trench, which would allow the jeep to pass without being damaged. As we gathered stones we prayed for our driver. His heart softened and he showed his gratitude for our willingness to collect stones to do the necessary repair. God's grace was drawing him into a new relationship with his Maker.

Praise be to the King of Kings and Lord of Lords, we arrived at Longlong after a tiring boneshaking journey. I wondered if the place got its name, because it was such a long, long way from anywhere else. We arrived without any damage to Jacob's jeepney, and he was a very happy man because he had fulfilled our wishes and his jeepney seemed none the worse for wear. For which we gave all the glory to God.

We were bruised and in need of a bath. I was now an expert at taking a bath Filipino mountain style. I thought nothing could shock or unnerve me, but I was in for a another surprise! As I walked around the village shaking hands with the men and embracing the women, I gradually acquired a trail of children. Slowly they overcame their shyness at the sight of this strange visitor with white skin. Although they were dressed in what Europeans would call rags, some were naked, and running barefoot over the rocky ground. They were as happy as little larks, full of smiles and hoots of joy. Their hair was matted and infested with lice, and their little hands could not help but scratch continuously, to relieve themselves of the itching pests.

I held out my arms showing that I wanted to give them a loving embrace. One little lad courageously stepped forward and held out his hand to me. I thought he wanted to shake hands. As I extended my hand to him, he took it and lifted it to his forehead. One by one the children came and greeted me in this fashion. Later I found out that this is the way Filipino children show respect to their elders.

The village was settling down to its evening routine, little fires were burning and the rice pots were simmering. The children left me to do their chores, and I stood looking around me surveying the scene. The surprise, which was about to shock me came with the sound of a loud honking noise directly behind me. Turning round, I saw a hissing fury of feathers with neck outstretched and flapping wings, heading straight for me. I quickly ran, with the yellow beak hissing and snapping at my heels.

The sight of the overdressed missionary, tearing around the village being persued by an angry gander and shouting, "Do something to get this wild bird off my tail, was ignored. Such a sight had never been seen before. All I could see were faces grinning from ear to ear, as I ran trying to get away from this ferocious monster bird. I fled past the Pastor, Jacob and my travelling companions. They were all laughing. Wherever I looked, I saw women, children, men – the entire village was in a state of hysterical laughter, so much so that they were doubled over with stitches. I could not see what was so funny, but I had to act in faith, and show this bird that I had dominion over him.

The headscarf that I used to protect my hair from the dust and grime of the journey was still round my neck. Grabbing the scarf, I did an abrupt about turn, and faced the gander head on, and whacked it over its beak with my scarf. At the same time I shouted, "In the name of Jesus Christ you will obey me." The angry hissing changed to an apologetic honking, and he continued to follow me at a respectable distance, then I said to him, "Get out of my sight. I do not want to see you. You have made a laughing stock of me in the sight of all the people." With a dejected honk he turned around and waddled away.

"Sister Chapman, he was only doing his duty. They have no dogs here, the geese are the watchdogs." said pastor Padua. Smiling sweetly with all the grace I could muster I asked, "Where can I take a bath?" I was trying very hard not to show that the incident made me feel that I was not one of them. My feeling was that of rejection.

Their faces dropped, when they realized that I was not happy about what had happened. As I took my bath Filipino style, I lifted my feelings before the Lord, and prayed in the Holy Ghost. I was here on the King's business, so decided that I must not allow this incident to cause a gap between the brethren and myself.

"Lord I forgive them!"

My thoughts were interrupted by Marilyn's voice.

"The meal is served, Sister Isabel."

"Thank you, I will be there in a minute."

All eyes were looking at me questioningly as I entered the room. With a beaming smile I said, "I am so hungry, hungry enough to eat that old bad tempered gander."

They smiled and the ice was broken!

"Sister Chapman, I am sorry, I should have done something to help you." said the Pastor very apologetically.

"Forget it. I have already forgiven you all."

But they were not ready to forget the incident. I could see that they were doing their best to stop grinning, and they started to recall the incident in English, so that I could understand what was being said. Finally I saw the scene from their perspective, and I started to laugh. Before we started the meal our entire company was once again in fits of laughter, including myself. The laughter healed the hurt and rejection, and I felt one with them again. Praise the Lord.

Sitting on the floor, eating with my fingers Filipino style, my eyes fixed on a peculiar object suspended above the door. Pointing to the object I asked, "What is that?"

"It is the skeleton of a snake."

"Is it only for decoration or does it have another purpose?"

Pastor Padua turned to enquire of our host. There followed a long conversation with much gesturing going on, concerning the purpose of the snake skeleton. In between mouthfuls of rice, the Pastor interpreted the conversation. "They believed that snakes cannot drown. On a journey that involved fording a river, our host wore the snake's skeleton on his head, so that the spirit of the snake would keep him safe."

I replied, "That is devilish superstition. He needs to renounce his trust in the spirit of a dead snake and destroy that skeleton. His faith for protection should be in the living Lord Jesus Christ, not in the skeleton of a dead snake."

When the meal was over I ministered to our host with the Pastor as my interpreter. He realized that it was indeed foolishness to trust in a dead skeleton, when we have a living Lord who watches over us. We led him in a prayer to renounce this superstitious belief. Then I laid hands on him and took authority over these superstitious demons that had deceived him, in the name of Jesus Christ. The moment of truth had come. If he was truly free he would be willing to destroy the snake skeleton. Looking directly into his eyes I said, "Are you willing to destroy the skeleton?"

Without hesitation he reached up and took it from its place above the door and handed it to me. "Please, you do it!"

I was left standing there with this satanic object of superstition in my hand.

"Pastor, please come with me and find out if anyone has a hammer." Outside a hammer was thrust into my hand, and with a whole crowd of people watching me, I threw the skeleton on the ground and proceeded to smash it into pieces. Then I picked up every last piece, and threw the smashed skeleton pieces into a fire that was still burning. The pieces ignited into an orange flame, and I prayed, "In the name of Jesus Christ, I bind the demons that were working through this snake skeleton. Please, Lord, send an angel of light to take these demons to the waiting place, to await the final judgment, when they will be cast into the lake of fire and brimstone." I believed it was accomplished in the spirit realm just as I had prayed.

The incident with the snake skeleton set the scene for my preaching that evening. The Pastor explained that many people were deeply involved in spiritism, superstition and witchcraft. There was not a hospital, doctor or dentist in the community, but there was a witchdoctor. The story was related to me as follows. "The sick person would give a chicken to the witchdoctor, which he killed and bled and sacrificed in a ritual ceremony. The sacrifice appeased the evil spirit, and the demon of sickness left the sick person, but only for a short time. The demon had a habit of returning and would afflict the individual with the same symptoms. The witch doctor demanded another chicken or piglet to sacrifice, before he would call off the afflicting demon, and so it went on."

Only the truth can set the captives free. These people needed to know that all demonic spirits must obey the name of the Lord Jesus Christ. I was not only going to tell them this wonderful truth, I would demonstrate it before their eyes.

Chapter Fifteen

I had learnt from past experience that demonic forces would interfere with a meeting where their evil works were being exposed. I began the meeting by binding the principalities and powers at work in that area, in the almighty name of Jesus Christ. Opening my bible I read from Ephesians 6:11-18, then proceeded as follows.

"Here on earth we are in a spiritual battle against demonic forces. Their only aim is to steal kill and destroy. When Jesus was here on earth he went about doing good, healing all who were oppressed of the devil. (Acts 10:38) This verse reveals to us that the majority of sickness and pain is demon oppression. The good news is Jesus defeated Satan and his evil fallen spirits two thousand years ago. Jesus has given believers the 'power of attorney' to use His name to command evil spirits of infirmity to loose their hold of their victims. Jesus commissioned his body to cast out devils and heal the sick, and even raise the dead.

Jesus came from Heaven to earth, being supernaturally conceived in a virgin's womb. His mission to earth was to destroy the works of the devil, and set fallen humanity free from sin's power to curse us with disease, suffering, poverty and eternal damnation. When Jesus came into our world, the entire population of the world, except for a handful of Jews, were under the rule and dominion of the devil, Satan. (Luke 4: 5-7) God's creation mankind were all under the power of the curse of the Law, suffering sickness and disease and headed towards damnation in the lake of fire and brimstone.

Jesus satisfied Divine Justice on behalf of fallen

humanity, by giving his own sinless body, to suffer the pain and agony of the stripes of the torturous scourge. As Jesus bore the pain and agony of the stripes, He was bearing our sickness and carrying our pain. The consequences of our sins were imputed (credited) to Jesus. He bore the pain and agony of the scourge, so that His health and life could be imputed to believers, as a gift of God's loving mercy and grace. He then died the cursed death of crucifixion in our stead. Our sins were imputed to Him, so that His righteousness could be imputed to us, as a gift of God's amazing grace towards fallen humanity. Thus Jesus redeemed believers from the curse of the law.

By merit of our Lord suffering the pain and agony of the scourge, His sacrificial death and holy redeeming blood, on our behalf, the ransom payment for sin was paid in full. Divine Justice accepted the sufferings and sacrificial death of Jesus, as the 'once and for all' perfect sacrifice for sin. Thus the devil lost his case against the redeemed of the Lord. The devil can no longer accuse, condemn and curse believers with disease and suffering or damn believers to the second death. The verdict stands, "Innocent. The price of sin is fully paid, therefore the consequences of sin are removed."

We have free choice as did Adam and Eve and the angels in heaven. Free to accept or reject God's offer. We can choose to graciously and gratefully respond to God's amazing grace, and accept the Lord Jesus Christ as our scapegoat, who suffered the agony of the scourge, to provide life and health for us. We can believe and accept Jesus as our sacrificial lamb, and receive our sins forgiven and annulled, through faith in the atonement in Christ's death and redeeming blood. We can receive the free gift of Christ's imputed righteousness, which gives us right standing with God. We are also free to reject Christ's suffering agony and pain of the stripes, which remove the curse of disease, pain and damnation from us. We are likewise free to reject the sacrifice of Jesus' death and blood to cancel out our sins.

No one can serve two masters. If we serve the risen Lord Jesus Christ we must renounce and turn away from all trust in superstitious objects, the witch doctor, in consulting the dead, praying to idols that are blind, deaf, dumb lifeless objects. God has given us a brain, and common sense tells us that an idol cannot hear or answer our prayers. We should not defy our own common sense and pray to a lifeless deaf, dumb, blind idol. There are demons of deception behind all forms of idolatry, which deceive individuals into doing that which is contrary to our mental sense and reasoning.

When mediums consult the dead, they are not talking to the spirit of our beloved dead relations, they are communicating with demons. When death takes a person, the spirit leaves the body of the dead corpse, and goes to one of two places, heaven or hell. No contact can be made with the spirits of the dead. A medium is a disciple of the devil, and a channel through which evil spirits impersonate the spirits of the dead. These demons have been around for a long time and are full of information. God has forbidden the practice of communicating with the dead, because it is direct communication with demons. Such a practice is an abomination in the sight of the One True Living God.

Anyone who has been involved in such evil satanic practices, must renounce them, and ask God's forgiveness, and forever turn away from that which God has forbidden. Anyone trusting in superstitious objects, must destroy all such emblems and ask Gods forgiveness, and forever turn away from such satanic practices. We should stop defying our own common sense, by bowing before and praying to dead, lifeless idols, which have a nose but no breath in them. We must not give offerings of any kind to dead idols, as it is giving offerings to demons. God looks upon idolaters as people who *hate* Him, because they do those things that violate the brain and common sense which God has created in us. (Exodus 20: 3-6)We must destroy all such despicable idols.

At the meeting I said, "The choice is yours! Tonight you must choose whose side you are on. If you choose the Lord Jesus Christ, you must be willing to destroy all superstitious objects and idols. To prove to God that your decision is genuine, and not just putting on a show, please go home and bring all those things in your homes which are displeasing to God. Then He will set you free from the curse of the Law, and impart eternal life to your spirit.

The gathered company made their way back to their homes, which were only minutes away. We prayed in the Holy Ghost and waited to see the result.

One by one they returned carrying idols, crucifixes, rosary beads and many other superstitious objects, and handed them to me. I threw them to the ground, and soon a pile of objects and idols lay heaped up in front of me. In the name of Jesus Christ I bound the demons at work behind these satanic objects, tied them up in spiritual chains, and rendered them powerless to continue to influence anyone under the sound of my voice.

I asked our Father in Heaven to dispatch his angels of light, to take the demons of darkness to the waiting place, to await the final judgment and face the lake of fire and brimstone. I then commanded all evil spirits of infirmity and pain, fever, and disease to leave the people, as they now understood and believed that Jesus Christ had redeemed them from the curse of the Law. I then led the congregation in a prayer of repentance, and they accepted Jesus as their sickness bearer and sin bearer - their Saviour.

One by one they got up and testified to their healing. I could not understand what they were saying, but the looks of joy that radiated from their faces revealed that they were very happy. I spotted Joseph, our driver, standing in the midst of the crowd, with head bowed joining in the prayer of repentance and receiving Jesus as his Saviour healer and sin bearer. The angels in heaven were rejoicing. The demons that were banished to hell were shaking with fear, dread and terror. They were confined, and could do no more evil to another person on earth. Their future was eternal torment with their leader Satan.

The men made a bonfire with the relics and idols, which still smoldered the following morning. Some more wood was added to cook the rice for breakfast, so every last part of the abominable things were burnt to ashes.

Pastor Padua would place a Pastor in Longlong to continue the work which we had begun, and in time they would build a native style fellowship building. Wandering around the village saying goodbye to my new found friends, I remembered the gander. Where was he? He had certainly kept well out of my way over the past few days. As we boarded the jeepney, he suddenly appeared and gave us a honking goodbye, which made every one erupt in laughter.

Palatong was our next destination. A Christian fellowship had already been established here, by the pastor and his co-workers. I felt the need to have communion and said so to our Pastor. During the conversation, I discovered that communion had never been celebrated at this relatively new Fellowship, because they did not understand 1Corinthians 11:29. They were frightened that they might come under the judgment of God, so decided not to have communion.

1 Corinthians 11: 29

For he that eats and drinks unworthily, eats and drinks judgment to himself, not discerning the Lord's body.

It was decided that I would preach on the subject and introduce the brethren to the Lord's Table. So we stopped and bought some grape juice and crackers. The enemy had done a good job of keeping the believers away from the bread and wine which are the elements of the Everlasting Covenant. The enemy used fear, of coming under the judgment of God, to prevent the new believers from eating and drinking at the Lord's Table. God has not given us the spirit of fear, but of love and of power and of a sound mind. Fear is a satanic tool of the devil which opposes faith.

The members had gathered in the church and the bread and wine was laid out on the altar in preparation for their first Communion Service. Our praise and worship leader began strumming on his guitar, and the entire congregation began to sing praises to our Lord. Suddenly, I began to cough and choke and instinctively put my hand on my throat. It felt as though my throat was on fire with burning coals. I could hardly breathe, and for a split second thought I would choke. I heard others behind me coughing, choking, spluttering, screaming and shrieking. I was amazed to see everyone holding their throats as if unseen hands were trying to choke the entire congregation to death. I was flabbergasted, shocked and horrified. My mind could not comprehend what was happening. There was a mad rush for the door and the Church was vacated in a matter of seconds. I heard blood curdling screams as if someone was in the throws of an agonizing death. Turning round I saw a young woman stretched out on the floor. Her agonizing screams and violent struggle to catch her breath, made it look as if she was having a seizure. I was bent over almost double, weak with the effort of coughing and gasping, in an attempt to draw breath into my lungs.

Suddenly I realized we were the only two left in the Church building.

I could not go and leave the young woman in her frenzied condition, and I could not pray as I had no breath to speak. God the Holy Ghost took over and I started praying in tongues within my spirit, and laid my hands on the girl. As I prayed in the Spirit my breathing became easier, and the girl was becoming calmer, the violent jerking movements were subsiding, and I noticed that it was no longer such a struggle for her to breathe. The cause of the problem was something in the air, which now seemed to be clearing. As I continued to pray for the young woman, I could hear loud, angry, shouting going on outside the Church door. It sounded as though a madman was in a fit of rage. The language barrier made it impossible for me to understand what was actually being said, but there was no mistaking the venom in the voice. I was aware of the fact that we were involved with a head on collision with the forces of darkness. Satan and his agents did not want us there, they did not want the congregation to understand the freely provided benefits of the everlasting Covenant, and had cleared the Church in a matter of seconds.

Pastor Padua had been outside trying to pacify the madman, but came back in to see if we were all right. He explained to me what had happened. When the congregation went out side to escape the choking, breath taking fumes, and breathe fresh air into their lungs, they were faced with a man pointing a rifle at them. He was yelling and cursing and shouting obscenities, and blaspheming the name of Jesus. He was totally out of control, driven by demons of hate, anger and unreasonable rage, which were aimed at the strangers who had arrived at the Church. The demons that possessed the madman, did not want us there, and decided to drive us out like wasps from their nest. He had ground up dried pepper and other harmful aromatic spices, wrapped his spicy concoction in a cloth, set fire to it and threw it into the building in the midst of the congregation.

The air fans dispersed the smoking ground pepper mixture throughout the Church. When inhaled it had very painful and frightening effects, which made everyone feel as though they were literally being choked to death. The demon-possessed madman was still outside the Church door shouting out obscenities and blaspheming the name of Jesus. He was threatening to shoot us, if we did not get back in the jeepney and leave Palatong. I spoke to the congregation who had come back inside the church to get away from the end of a pointed rifle. I explained that Jesus had given believers power and authority over all devils. We joined hands in the bond of unity, and I prayed, and bound the demons that were working through the madman. They were using a gun, a violent temper and fear to try and drive us away. In the name of Jesus Christ of Nazareth, we rendered the demons powerless to continue the attack against us. We were not going to be moved. They had to obey the name of our Lord. The brethren agreed with a hearty, "Amen."

Within thirty minutes the air in the church building was cleared of the harmful fumes, the demon-possessed madman had left without using his rifle, and the meeting resumed as if the incident had just been a bad nightmare. The Pastor went to the platform and opened the Service for a second time. He began with a prayer of thanksgiving to the Lord, that we had all overcome the recent ordeal, none the worse for the satanic attack. He also prayed for the salvation of the demon possessed man. He then went on to address the congregation, and encourage them to listen to the preaching of the word, which would dispel all fear concerning partaking of the bread and wine at the Lord's Table.

This would be a very special meeting, which would be blessed by God's power and presence, as it was their first celebration of Holy Communion. As he spoke I opened my Bible and it was as if 1Corinthians 10:20-21 was highlighted, and standing out of the page. The Holy Ghost knew what was needful to set the captives free to serve the Lord Jesus, and was leading me by the power of his indwelling Spirit. To be perfectly honest, I must have read this particular scripture before, but it had not registered with me, until that precise second.

But I say, that the things which the gentiles sacrifice, they sacrifice to devils, and not to God: and I would not that ye should have fellowship with devils. Ye cannot drink the cup of the Lord, and the cup of devils: ye cannot be partakers of the Lord's table, and the table of devils. (1 Cor 10:20-21)

I had barely finished reading the scripture, when I realized that the Pastor was introducing me to the congregation. In the few seconds that it took for me to take my place behind the lectern, God had revealed to me that there were some present who were involved in giving sacrifices to idols. Addressing the congregation I said, "God has revealed to me that there are some present who are involved in giving sacrifices to idols, which in actual fact is giving sacrifices to devils. We cannot hide anything from Almighty God, He sees and hears and knows all things. If you give offerings to idols, whether it is flowers, food, fruit or sweets you are giving sacrifices to devils. If you give offerings of food or drink to the spirits of the dead, you are sacrificing to devils. If you give offerings to a witchdoctor you are giving sacrifices to devils." (I was learning that all such things were common practices, with those who were not familiar with the teaching of God's word).

"Thus says the Lord God Almighty, You cannot drink the cup of the Lord and the cup of devils: you cannot be partakers of the Lords table and the table of devils.

If you are involved in such religious rituals, please come forward and renounce these satanic practices now. Almighty God has clearly stated, "You cannot drink the cup of the Lord and at the same time give sacrifices to devils. You cannot be partakers at the Lord's Table and the table of devils. We cannot allow you to come to the Covenant Table if you are giving sacrifices and offerings to idols, or the spirits of the dead, or the witchdoctor. You cannot fellowship with devils, and at the same time have Holy Communion at the Lord's table. If you want to enter into Covenant relationship with God, you must be willing to renounce such satanic practices and ask God's forgiveness."

I waited, believing that the Holy Spirit would convict those involved in such sin. There was an uncanny hush in the place, and two people got up and walked out. They had made their decision to stick with serving the devil through idols, or serving devils through giving offerings to the dead. They had chosen to reject the Lord and his Table to follow pagan practices. Everyone is free to make their own choice and decision.

I continued to wait, feeling sure that others would respond. Suddenly, I realised that a tremendous battle was going on in the minds and hearts of certain individuals. The uncanny hush continued and every one sat perfectly still as if glued to their seats. The indwelling Holy Ghost prompted me to pray and take authority over the evil spirits that were ruling over those who prayed to idols and statues, and gave offerings to the dead and the witchdoctor. "In the name of the Lord Jesus Christ, I bind all idolatrous demons of darkness, demons of witchcraft, demons of superstition and spiritism and render you powerless to influence the decisions of those under the sound of my voice."

Sighs of relieve were audibly heard around the congregation. It appeared that they wanted to make the right decision and come to the Lord's Table, but were being held back by something they did not understand. The prayer, released the congregation from the devil's bondage, and the uncanny hush was once more broken as a young couple rose to their feet, and started to move in my direction. All over the congregation people began to rise from their chairs and come forward for ministry. One individual said, "We do not pray to idols, we pray to God through idols." After explaining that Jesus was the only mediator between God and mankind, each individual renounced their particular sin of consorting with demons and praying to idols. Some of these sins included offering sacrifices to idols, praying to the dead, and for the dead, involvement with witchdoctors and many of their other superstitious beliefs that I had never heard of. Having renounced their demon involvement I prayed again, bound and commanded the oppressing demons to loose their hold of the people, through faith in the power of the name of Jesus Christ.

The events that then took place revealed that they had indeed been set them free from satanic bondages. One man joyfully cried out;

"My arthritic pains are gone." He was bending and stretching and lifting up his knees without pain. A woman said, "I have been cursed with headaches for as long as I can remember. The pain in my head is gone." It appeared that everyone was testifying of being set free from various complaints, pains and diseases. That was quite a start to the meeting, and was totally led by the Lord who never fails to amaze me. Once the people were seated again I continued my address.

Opening my Bible I read 1Corinthians 11:24-26. The bread and wine are the elements or symbols of the Everlasting Covenant that God has made with us through all the suffering, sacrificial death, resurrection and ascension of our Lord Jesus. A Covenant is a mutual agreement. This means it takes two parties to make it work effectively. God 'in Christ' perfectly fulfilled His side of the Covenant agreement, therefore God is bound by His word, to keep and fulfil His side of the Covenant contract.

We as individuals must keep our side of the Covenant agreement, which is a matter of faith, based on all that Jesus has freely provided in the atonement. First we need to know and understand what the elements of the Covenant symbolise. Then we have to know and understand what the benefits of the Covenant are, and take them by faith, based in the promises of God's word. Without faith it is impossible to please God. The Covenant meal imparts to us all that Jesus has freely provided for believers in the atonement.

Atonement: reconciliation of sinners with God through Jesus' sufferings, sacrificial death and holy redeeming blood, His resurrection and ascension.

All Jesus' sufferings and sacrificial death are 'laid out before us' in the Covenant meal. The bread is the spiritual substance, or is symbolic of our Lord's body, which was broken for us, by whose stripes we were healed. The wine is the spiritual substance, or is symbolic of Christ's holy redeeming blood.

John 6: 53 – 56

Then Jesus said unto them, Verily, verily I say unto you, Except ye eat the flesh of the Son of man, and drink his blood, ye have no life in you.

Whosoever eateth my flesh, and drinketh my blood,

hath eternal life; and I will raise him up at the last day.

For my flesh is meat indeed, and my blood is drink indeed.

He that eateth my flesh, and drinketh my blood, dwelleth in me, and I in him.

The above scripture is not talking about transubstantiation, whereby priests claim to have the power to turn the bread and wine into the actual blood and body of Jesus. That is a pagan concept which incorporates cannibalism.

The wine we drink, and the bread we eat, at the Lord's Table, is the spiritual substance of all the blessings which Jesus' sufferings, death and holy redeeming blood, freely purchased for us. The bread and the wine, is our spiritual food. Jesus is the true vine. Believers are the branches. We have to eat our spiritual food in order to draw life, health, strength and power to produce fruit. In the same way as the natural branch draws sap from the trunk, which provides it with nourishment, in our daily lives believers must eat and drink spiritual food to maintains life, health, strength and power to produces the fruit of the Spirit, as well as the fruit of the atonement. If we cut off the natural branch from its trunk, the branch and the fruit it was bearing will wither and die. In the same way, believers must eat and drink our spiritual food to maintain life, health, strength and enabling power to produce the fruit of the Spirit, as well as the fruit of the atonement in our daily lives.

The bread and wine symbolise, or is the spiritual substance of all the blessings of the Everlasting Covenant, which have been freely provided for us, and are as follows:

Of primary importance is deliverance out of Satan's kingdom. This comes about by means of the new birth, and the regenerating power of the indwelling Holy Ghost. When we are born again, we are delivered out of Satan's kingdom of darkness and are translated into the kingdom of God, and become members of Christ's body. We are united with God, by the indwelling Holy Ghost. The Holy Ghost performs the miracle of regeneration, which transforms our spirit into the image and likeness of Jesus. Our regenerate spirit is created in righteousness and true holiness, possessing eternal life, and cannot sin, because it is born of the incorruptible seed of God. Our born again spirit is a new creation, a brand new man.

Col 1: 12-14

Giving thanks to the Father, which hath made us meet to be partakers of the inheritance of the saints of light: Who hath delivered us from the power of darkness,and hath translated us into the Kingdom of his own dear son: In whom we have redemption through his blood, even the forgiveness of sins.

Secondly our sins are forgiven. Jesus gave His sinless life to pay the full ransom payment for the sins of the world. We are the guilty sinners, who should have faced the death penalty for violating God's Law. Jesus died as our substitute. Our sins were imputed to Him, set down to His account. Jesus chose to die the death of a common criminal in our place. In Jesus day, criminals were brutally scourged with an instrument of torture, and then faced the death penalty by crucifixion, to pay the penalty for crimes committed. Having suffered the agony of the scourge and the humiliation of death by crucifixion, Jesus died on Calvary's tree, as the Lamb of God to take away the sins of the world. His body was bled, to provide the blood for the atonement, which cancelled out our sin record. The Roman soldier pierced his side with a spear, and Jesus body was drained of blood and water. Thus, Christ Jesus paid the full ransom payment for the sins of the world. He was the sinless Lamb of God who took away the sins of the world –

annulled the power and consequences of sin, that was against us.

1John 3: 4-5

Whosoever commits sin transgresses the law: for sin is the

transgression of the law. And you know that he was manifested

to take away our sins; and in him is no sin.

The good news of the gospel of the grace of God is that your sins have been forgiven. Not only forgiven, but abolished - annulled. Our sins were nailed to Calvary's tree with the death of Christ. Not just some sin, but all sin, this includes your past, present and even your future sins. As we drink from the cup of the Covenant, we enter into communion with the blood of Jesus. We confess our trespasses and receiving our forgiveness, knowing and believing that the death and blood of Jesus, has paid the full ransom price and annulled our sin record. Our sins were imputed to Jesus, so that His righteousness could be imputed to us. Therefore we cast off our garments that are stained with sin, and clothe ourselves by faith with Christ's robe of imputed righteousness.

Unto Him that loved us, and washed us from our sins in His own blood. (Rev 1: 5)

For he (God) hath made him (Christ) to be sin for us, who knew no sin; that we be made the righteousness of God in him. (2 Cor 5:21)

Jesus was made sin for us. This means a sin-offering. The sins of the world were imputed to Jesus, charged to his account, as He died the horrendous death of crucifixion, as our substitute sin offering. So that Christ's righteousness could be imputed to believers.

Imputed means: set down to the account of one to whom it does not belong - credited to.

Righteousness is the free gift of God. Believers are the righteousness of God, "in Christ Jesus", by faith in the substitute death of Christ and His holy atoning blood. Our sins were imputed to Jesus, that His righteousness be imputed to believers.

As we commune with the blood of Jesus and drink from the cup of the Covenant, we clothe ourselves with the robe of righteousness which Jesus' blood freely purchased and provided for us, by faith. The believer's righteousness is faith righteousness, based on the atonement in Jesus' death and redeeming blood. Believers leave the Covenant Table cleansed of all sin and clothed with the garment of righteousness, which Jesus' death and holy redeeming blood freely provided for us. This is a matter of faith.

For with the heart man believeth unto righteousness; and with the mouth confession is made unto salvation. (Rom 10:10)

The believer's right standing with God is a matter of what we believe in our heart and confess with our mouth. With the heart, we believe that we are the righteousness of God in Christ Jesus. We are convinced of this wonderful truth, by the convicting power of the Holy Ghost through the written word of God. Jesus loved us and washed us from our sins in His own blood. (Rev 1: 5)

We must abide in Jesus, the true vine, and live by grace through faith in what His atonement has freely provided for us. It is not a case of "trying to be like Jesus". By our efforts, we could never match the perfect righteousness of Jesus. It is a case of being who we are <u>in</u> Christ Jesus, by grace through faith. Jesus death saved us from the second death. By merit of his death on our behalf, Jesus imparts eternal life to our regenerate spirit.

1John 4: 9

In this was manifested the love of God towards us,

because that God sent his only begotten Son, *that we might live through him.*

How do we live <u>through</u> Jesus?

Jesus is the true vine, and we are the branches. The branches draw their life, health, strength and power to produce fruit, through living <u>in</u> and <u>through</u> the sap of the main trunk. We abide in the vine by living by faith in all the blessings which Jesus' atonement freely provided for us.

We live in and through Jesus by grace through faith. We live by faith in all the blessings that he has freely provided for us in the atonement. Namely;

We were saved by His grace.

We were delivered out of the kingdom of darkness by His indwelling Holy Spirit.

We will never face the wrath of God, because Jesus' death satisfied Divine Justice on our behalf.

We possess eternal life in our regenerate spirit, because His Spirit lives in us.

We were cleansed of all sin and forgiven, because His death and blood paid the ransom price to abolish our sin record.

We are no longer being charged with the sins of our flesh, our sin record was abolished for all time, by the redeeming blood of Jesus.

We are righteous with His imputed righteousness.

We were healed by His stripes.

We can do the same works Jesus' did, because he imparted to us the measure of His faith. We can do all things through Christ who strengthens us.

We live <u>in</u> Jesus, by faith in all He has freely provided for us in the atonement.

John 15: 4-6

Jesus said, "Abide in me, and I in you. As the branch cannot bear fruit of itself, except it abide in the vine; no more can ye, except ye abide in me.

I am the vine, ye are the branches: He that abideth in me, and I in him, the same bringeth forth much fruit: for without me ye can do nothing.

As we eat and drink the elements of the everlasting Covenant, we abide in the vine and He abides in us. There is a twin aspect to the atonement in Christ Jesus. The bread and the wine, symbolise the twin aspects of the atonement. The wine symbolises the death and blood of Jesus. His death satisfied divine justice on our behalf, and paid the ransom price to set us free from being judged for our transgressions. His blood atoned for sin and abolished, annulled our sin record. Once and for all, and for all time.

The bread we eat at the Covenant Table, is the spiritual substance, or symbolizes the body of Jesus that was broken for us, by whose stripes we WERE healed.

The broken body of Jesus provided physical healing for this life, and a new glorified body in the coming eternal spiritual world, for all believers. The hand of faith can only reach out and take, that which the eye of faith sees to be a free provision of the Covenant. Before we can receive our healing at the Lord's Table, we must be totally convinced by God's word, that healing is a free provision of the atonement in Christ Jesus. Any shadow of doubt or unbelief will rob us of our healing.

That it might be fulfilled which was spoken by Esaias the prophet, saying, Himself took our infirmities, and bare our sicknesses. (Matt 8:17)

Our means our. Jesus took our infirmities and bore our sicknesses, to set us free from the curse of the law – pain, suffering, disease, poverty and the second death. How did Jesus bear our infirmities and sicknesses? Our Lord's body was broken for our healing. He endured the pain and the agony of the cruel scourge. We do not know how many torturous lashes of the scourge Jesus endured as our scapegoat. The Jews stopped at thirty nine lashes, as punishment for crimes committed by criminals. Forty was their count. However they stopped after the thirty ninth stripe, in case of a miscount. Jesus was scourged and striped by the Romans, who were not under the moderation of Jewish Law. Therefore we do not know how many torturous stripes Jesus bore as our scapegoat, to set us free from the curse of the law. Jesus was cursed for our transgressions. He bore the punishment of our crimes, to set us free from the 'curse of the Law'. He gave his back to the smiters and those who brutally tore the beard off his face. Jesus was treated as a common criminal. He was mocked, abused, spat upon, and bore the torture of the scourge, which made deep furrows in His human flesh. Thus Jesus bore our sicknesses and carried our pains, to save redeemed believers from the curse of the Law.

Isaiah 50: 6

I gave my back to the smiters and my cheeks to them that plucked off the hair: I hid not my face from shame and spitting.

Jesus fulfilled the symbolism of the scapegoat, which was led out in to the wilderness bearing and removing the curse of the law, from God's chosen people the Jews. Jesus also fulfilled the symbolism of the sacrificial animals that were put to death and bled as a substitute sin offering, as practiced under the type and shadow of the Old Covenant. (See Leviticus chapter 16).Why did Jesus choose to endure the stripes of the scourge as a common criminal? To set us free from the curse of the Law - sickness, suffering, disease, poverty and damnation. By whose stripes we were healed. The healing which Jesus stripes freely purchased for us is both physical and spiritual.

We have the first fruits of our redemption now, in this

life, regardless of the fact, that sin is still lodged in our corruptible flesh. We are the righteousness of God in Christ Jesus. Our sins were imputed to Jesus that his righteousness be imputed to us.

Regardless of the fact that our mortal flesh grows old, we were healed by the Lord's stripes, and can maintain good health even in our old age. It is a case of abiding in the vine, and living in good health and glorifying God in our body. Within our temple dwells the Spirit of Christ, in the secret place of the Holy of Holies within us.

Death is not punishment for sin. The price of sin was fully paid by our sacrificial Lamb, our Lord Jesus Christ. Death to the true believer is gain. The mortal body must be laid down in death, so that our born again spirit can be clothed in immortality.

The healing which the Lord's stripes bought and paid for was physical healing for this life and a glorified immortal body in the coming eternal kingdom. Both were bought and paid for, by the Lord's suffering the agony of the scourge on behalf of fallen humanity. The only way we can receive both physical healing for here and now, and a glorified body in the coming kingdom, is through faith in the promises of God's word. Jesus' stripes, death and redeeming blood, annulled the power of the curse of the law that was against us.

Jesus is the bread of life. As we eat the bread at the Lord's Table, we commune with the body of Jesus, which was broken and lashed, to set us free from the curse of the law. We receive our physical healing and maintain our eternal life by faith, based on the promises of God's word. Jesus was both our sin-bearer and sickness- bearer. He was our 'sacrificial lamb' and our 'scapegoat'.

Who his own self bare our sins in his own body on the tree, (as he died the cursed death of crucifixion by giving

His life as the perfect ransom payment for sin) that we, being dead to sin, (sin has lost its power to condemn and damn us) should live unto righteousness: (walk in Christ's imputed righteousness by faith) by whose stripes we were healed,. Both spiritually and physically. (1 Peter 2: 24).

As we eat the bread at the Covenant Table, we commune with the body of Jesus and eat the bread of life and health by faith. As Jesus bore the agony of the stripes in His own living body, He was bearing our sicknesses and carrying our pains. The 'consequences' of our sins were imputed to Jesus. What were the consequences of sin that Jesus bore as our substitute? Surely it was sickness, pain, suffering, poverty and the second death – the curse of the Law. Christ hath, past tense, redeemed us from the curse of the law. (Gal 3:13)

As we, the branches, eat the bread of life and health at the Lord's Table, we draw the sap of life, health, strength and provision from Christ, the true vine.

The curse of the law was imputed to Jesus, that His life, health, strength and provision, be imputed to us by grace through faith.

As we eat the bread of life in faith, the life, health strength, power and provision which Jesus stripes purchased for us, is imputed to us.

The curse of the Law was imputed to Jesus as our scapegoat, because He bore the torture of the scourge, so that His life, health, strength, power and abundance is imputed to us.

By faith we exchange our sicknesses, weaknesses, failures and lack, for Christ's life, health, strength, power and abundance.

Our God has promised to provide all our needs according to his riches in Glory by Christ Jesus. We take our abundant provision by faith, wholeheartedly believing that God will provide all our needs, based on the promises of His word.

When we eat and drink at the Lord's Table, we are like the branches of the natural vine that draws its life and well-being from the trunk.

As we eat the bread of life, we should believe that it is God's will to prosper us, and receive our prosperity by faith based on the promises of God's word. All in Christ are the seed of Abraham. Father Abraham was not a poor man. He was very rich and walked in the blessings of God.

The blood of the Covenant provides a shield of protection around us, in the same way as the Israelites were protected from the death angel, when the first born of every Egyptian child and beast, died in the night.

As we drink from the cup of the Covenant which symbolises, or is the spiritual substance of the blood of Jesus, we also take our divine protection by faith based on the promises of God's word.

(Isaiah 54:17)

No weapon that is formed against thee shall prosper; and every tongue that shall rise against thee in judgment thou shalt condemn. This is the heritage of the servants of the Lord, and *their righteousness is of me*, saith the Lord.

"Their righteousness is of me," saith the Lord. The redeemed of the Lord are righteous by faith, with Christ's imputed righteousness.

In Christ Jesus, we have eternal Life and a new glorified body. We possess eternal life now in our regenerate spirit. Our regenerate spirit will be clothed in a new glorified body. Even though we die, we know we will live forever in the eternal City, in the presence of our God. Faith is the substance of things hoped for, the evidence of things not seen. Faith in God's word brings the reality of the promise into existence. The just live by faith!

Living in and through Jesus – abiding in the true vine, is the life which the redeemed of the Lord must live, to produce the fruit of the Spirit and the blessings of the atonement in our daily lives.

My sheep hear my voice, and I know them, and they follow me: And I give unto them eternal life; and they shall never perish; neither shall any man pluck them out of my hand. (John 10: 27-28)

No man or demon can pluck us out of our Father's hand. According to Jesus' promise who is the author and finisher of our faith, we are eternally secure in Christ Jesus the rock of our salvation. Jesus is the authour and finisher of our faith. The work he has begun in us, He will bring to completion. Born again believers are sealed with the Holy Spirit of promise until the day of redemption. That glorious day, when we shall see Jesus face to face, and when we see him, we shall be like him, clothed in immortality. Then our redemption will be completed and perfected. Hallelujah!

Both physical healing for life here and now and a glorified body in the coming kingdom are integral parts of our salvation. Both were freely provided in the atonement in Christ Jesus our Lord and Saviour.

It is of vital importance that we do not eat and drink at the Lord's Table in ignorance or unbelief. We must eat and drink with full understanding and faith.

Wherefore whosoever shall eat this bread, and drink this cup of the Lord unworthily, shall be guilty of the blood and the body of the Lord. (1Cor 11: 27)

We must discern by the power of the Holy Ghost, what the word *"unworthily"* means in this verse of scripture. The word 'unworthily' means: not worthy, worthless, without value or merit. This verse of scripture is not talking about the "condition of the participant". This is referring to the participants understanding or opinion, of the bread and wine. We have no holiness or righteousness of our own that God can accept. God only accepts perfect holiness. Jesus was the only human being that walked in sinless perfection from birth to death. He perfectly kept the Ten Commandments on our behalf and gave his sinless body, as the "once for all" perfect sin-offering to satisfy Divine Justice and save believers from the curse of the Law, which is sickness, pain, disease, poverty and eternal damnation (Gal 3:13).

It is taught and believed by some, that we can only approach the Covenant Table if we are living a holy life. Those who think and believe along these lines are walking in filthy rags of self-righteousness – a fig leaf covering. Religion has perverted the meaning of the Covenant Table to embrace a false 'good works' gospel. If it were possible for fallen humanity to achieve a level of holiness which God could accept, by our own merit, Christ need not have died to save sinners. The Covenant Table is the place where redeemed believers (who continue to have sin lodged in our mortal flesh) meet with our Saviour, whereby we abide in the vine, and maintain the blessings of the atonement, through faith in the terms of the Covenant contract. The Covenant Table, is for all who have fallen short of the glory of God, which includes everyone. Even after we are born again, our flesh falls short of perfect righteousness. We will never maintain perfect righteousness in our mortal flesh. One example is, "Whatsoever is not of faith is sin." How often have we doubted God's ability to fulfill the promises of His word, and fallen short of His best for us through the sin of unbelief?

To eat and drink the elements of the Everlasting Covenant *'unworthily'* is to eat and drink as a mere religious rite, with no true understanding or faith involved. Those who eat and drink 'unworthily,' eat and drink in ignorance and unbelief, and do not understand the full symbolism and provision of the bread and wine. Therefore they are unable to receive the blessings, because of a lack of knowledge which breeds unbelief. Faith comes through knowledge of God's word, where there is little or no knowledge concerning the symbolism and provision of the everlasting Covenant, faith is not present to receive the blessings. Without faith it is impossible to please God.

The word 'unworthily' has nothing whatsoever to do with the condition of the participant. We are all unworthy sinners who deserve nothing from our holy God. God has chosen by His amazing mercy, grace and love, to bless believers and set us free from the curse, which sin brought upon the human race. When we eat and drink at the Covenant Table with *no true understanding or faith*, we are guilty of denying the body and blood of the Lord. Jesus sufferings and death are of no value to those who eat and drink 'unworthily' in ignorance and unbelief.

But let a man examine himself, and so let him eat of that bread and drink of that cup. 1 Cor 11: 28.

Let us examine ourselves, and see ourselves as we really are in the flesh. In our flesh dwells no good thing. We have all sinned and fallen short of the glory of God, so say the scriptures. If we say we have no sin we are liars and the truth is not in us. Even born again believers have a drive to sin, as the flesh serves the law of sin. We are to examine ourselves and face up to the truth – I am a redeemed sinner saved by God's mercy and grace, yet my flesh continues to fall short of my goal. Without a Saviour, we are headed towards eternal damnation. Before we drink from the cup of the Covenant, we must confess our sins, and by faith receive our forgiveness. We have to see our sins *imputed* to our sacrificial Lamb. We have to see His righteousness *imputed* to us as individuals. We have to know and believe with the whole heart, that the death and holy redeeming blood of Jesus paid the full ransom payment to set us free from the curse of the Law, which includes the second death - eternal torment in the lake of fire and brimstone.

As long as we live in our mortal body we live in two realms.We are both sinful and righteous at the same time. We are sinful in our flesh, in our flesh dwells no good thing. The things which we do not want to do, we find ourselves doing. The good that we should do, we do not always do. Yet, at the same time we are the righteousness of God in Christ Jesus. We were saved by grace through faith, and must daily live by grace through faith.

Another vital point that we need to understand before approaching the Covenant Table is that God can only forgive us, if we forgive those who have done us an injustice and hurt us. If we do not forgive, God will not forgive us our trespasses. If we do not forgive we will remain under the curse of the Law. (Mark 11: 25-26, Matt 6:14 & Col 3:13)

For he that eateth and drinketh unworthily, eateth and drinketh judgment to himself, not discerning the Lord's body. For this cause many are weak and sickly among you and many sleep. (have died) 1Cor 11: 29-30.

Those who eat and drink the bread and wine at the Lord's Table 'unworthily' with no true understanding and faith, bring judgment upon themselves. The judgment we bring upon ourselves is the curse of the Law. Many are weak and sick and have died a premature death, because they did not *discern* the Lord's body. We must *discern* the Lord's body. Distinguish between the Lord's body and blood. Discern means: make out, distinguish. There is a vital distinction between the benefits provided by the bread and wine at the Covenant Table. We must discern the twin aspects of the atonement in Christ Jesus, discern between

His blood and His body. The wine in the Covenant cup symbolises the death and blood of Jesus, which paid the full penalty for all our sins, and annulled our sin record. The bread we eat symbolises the body of Jesus that was brutally scourged, as he bore the curse of the law as our substitute.

God has declared that He has made a way to forgive all our sins and heal all our diseases. (Psalm 103) The prophet Isaiah said, "Who can believe our report?"

For this cause many are weak and sickly among you, and many sleep. (1 Cor 11: 30)

For this cause or reason many believers are weak and sick and have died a premature death. The reason or cause is because they did not discern the distinction between the Lord's body and blood – the bread and the wine. Therefore there was no understanding and faith present when they ate the bread, whereby they could receive their healing. Regardless of this truth, their faith in the death and blood of Jesus to cancel out their sins and save them from damnation was their passport home to glory. Praise him for His amazing grace.

1 Corinthians 10: 16

The cup of blessings which we bless, is it not the communion of the blood of Jesus Christ? The bread which we break, is it not the communion of the body of Christ?

Communion means, a 'coming together' between mutual parties, to have free passage from one to another. When we eat the bread at the Covenant Table we enter into communion with the body of Jesus, and a mutual exchange take place.

Through the eye of faith we see the curse of the law *imputed* to Jesus, as He bore the agony of the stripes as our substitute. Through the eye of faith we see the curse removed from us, and receive the imputed life, health, strength, power and provision which the stripes of Jesus freely provided for us.

When we drink from the cup of the Covenant we enter into communion with the death and holy redeeming blood of Jesus, and a mutual interchange of transactions takes place. Through the eye of faith we see our sins *imputed* to Jesus, as He died as our sacrificial Lamb and was bled to perfectly atone for all our sins. Through the eye of faith we see Jesus righteousness *imputed* to us as a gift of God's amazing grace. We exchange our sins, guilt and condemnation, for the righteousness which Jesus' blood freely purchased and provided for us by faith. Through the eye of faith, we see ourselves clothed in the robe of Christ's imputed righteousness.

We also receive the divine protection, which the blood of Jesus freely provides for his Covenant keeping saints. We also know that we will never come under the judgment of God, because the suffering and sacrificial death of Jesus, disarmed the power of the curse that was against us. We confirm our side of the Covenant contract by receiving all the freely provided blessings of the Everlasting Covenant by faith, based on the promises of God's word."

One by one the congregation came to the altar and ate the bread and drank from the cup at the Lord's Table, and entered into Covenant relationship with the Holy One of Israel. They left the Lord's Table clothed in robes of righteousness, having received their healing and all the blessings which the Everlasting Covenant freely affords. Even the little children were moved and touched by God's awesome presence, and came and ate and drank with understanding and faith. As the children came forward to partake of the bread and wine, the Holy Ghost spoke to my spirit and said, "Suffer little children, and forbid them not, to come unto me: for of such is the kingdom of heaven. (Matt 19: 14)

The congregation at Palatong was set free to walk in all the blessings of the Everlasting Covenant, and many testified of their healing in the evening meeting, including a little girl who had a speech impediment and was made perfectly whole. Her mother cried with tears of joy. Prior to that meeting we had a religious concept that the Covenant Table was only for grown-ups, but we saw that little children can come into knowledge and understanding of the benefits of the Covenant, and can receive from the Lord at His Table by faith. Children have no preconceived religious traditions and unbelief to stand in their way.

Chapter Sixteen

I awoke with a tremendous feeling of anticipation for today was the day that we planned to go back to the mountains of Kalinga Apayao. The preaching of the Gospel was slowly but surely breaking the pagan tradition of headhunting. Pastor Padua reckoned that the journey would take about fifteen hours. I tried not to think about it. God's grace and power got me there last time, and His grace and power would also be sufficient for this trip. Another white woman was going to accompany me for approximately ten days. Betty was her name. She was a big lady from America, who wanted to go and see some of these outlying places for herself. She did not know what she was letting herself in for, but God's grace would be sufficient for her, as it had been for me.

By nightfall we still had about fifty miles to travel. Pastor Alex, who frequently cheered us up by strumming on his guitar and leading us in praise choruses, decided instead to inject rather a gloomy note into the silence. In his broken English he said, "Very dangerous area this, sister Isabel. Much NPA hanging around in hideouts up here, bad place for ambush, nobody rides car here at night, too much frightened of kill and rob." That would be the reason why our vehicle was the only one on the road since darkness fell. Betty, we were finding out, was quite a character, and she leaned over and whispered with a note of anxiety in her voice, "I wish he hadn't told us that."

"The Lord's angels are with us. All is well." I reassured her.

The words were barely out of my mouth, when we saw

the headlights of a vehicle approaching from behind. It was moving faster than we were and covering the steep rise at high speed. It would soon overtake us. If the locals were too terrified to venture out at night, who were these? Were they on a long trip as we were, or were they cruel robbers and killers with a much more sinister purpose? The anxiety that we had felt since darkness fell, curled itself round us as our imaginations began to toy with thoughts of headhunters, armed rebels and robbers.

The danger of our location felt very real. In this sort of situation national characteristics begin to show. The Filipinos kept their thoughts to themselves and remained quiet. Betty was quite open about her fears and at the same time tried to make light of it. This became more difficult as the other vehicle closed the gap between us, causing the tension to grow. Only Betty managed to speak, "What do you think they will do to us?"

At that moment, I had the oddest reaction and burst out laughing, and then Betty was laughing. Marilyn was laughing. Our whole company, even the men were roaring out with laughter. Brother Alex has a very serious nature and to see him laughing in this way turned me on even more. I was in stitches doubled over with laughter, which seemed to break all the tension and fear. The headlights behind us were only a few feet away from our bumper. Our jeepney had no back door or windows which we could shut to protect ourselves. The occupants of the truck behind could clearly see us. All the onlookers in the vehicle behind could see we were a body of people in a bout of hysterical laughter. The laughter subsided as Betty brought us back into the reality of our situation.

"Why are they sticking so close to us?" asked Betty, with a twinge of fear in her voice. No one chose to answer her question, and a hushed silence filled the Jeepney, as everyone was busy with their own thoughts and silent prayers. The vehicle stole closer and closer to our bumper. We had to avert our eyes as their headlights were shining right into our faces. The occupants of the approaching vehicle were obviously having a good look at us. Suddenly, the vehicle behind pulled out to overtake us, and we could see that it was a pick-up truck. It drew level and we held our breath in anticipation. It was in no hurry to overtake us, the road up ahead was clear, so there was no reason for them to be hanging back and driving along beside us. For some minutes the truck drove alongside us and we could see that the trailer was covered by a waterproof tarpaulin.

"Do you think they are carrying guns under that tarpaulin?" Betty asked, revealing her inward thoughts. Once again her question remained unanswered, and I began to pray in the Spirit to overcome the spirit of fear that was once again beginning to affect our company. To our great relief, the driver of the truck speeded up and we watched the rear lights disappear over the brow of the hill. "Hallelujah! I praise you Lord for your divine protection." I exclaimed.

Betty's voice once again broke the silence, "Do you think they have stopped up ahead to set up an ambush?" I could not contain myself and burst into another fit of laughter with tears rolling down my cheeks. My infectious laugh got everyone else going, and our vehicle seemed to rock and roll along the road as our driver sought to control the wheel in between great peals of hilarious laughter.

"Please Betty, don't make another remark like that. My sides can't handle it."

We did not see the pick up again. By the grace of God we arrived safely at our destination. Our base was with Pastor Teckney and his wife who were now retired, their ministry being carried on by their children. Pastor Teckney looked leaner than I remembered. He seemed to have lost some of his joy, and I wondered what was bothering him.

The following morning we sat down to discuss our itinerary with Pastor Teckney, as he knew the area better than anyone else. "Sister Chapman, things are much worse than when you were here on your last visit. My brother-in-law was brutally murdered by members of the Bute-Bute tribe less than a year ago. During your last visit, we verged on the boundary that belongs to the Bute Bute tribe, and we all came back alive by the grace of God. To go back into that area at this time would be suicidal." Taking a deep breath he continued, "The New Peoples Army is now armed with rifles and they have recruited men from the headhunting tribes. They have taught the tribal men how to use rifles so they are also armed. Their rifles have been smuggled into our country, and have the long range capability of cutting a person down in death, at long distances. Nowadays there are army checkpoints in the mountains, fighting against the rebels and the headhunters. The headhunters, who have not yet been reached with the gospel, no longer remove the head of their victims. A head is too big to conceal at the check point areas. They now cut off ears or fingers, and bring them back to their villages as a trophy to prove their manhood.

My brother-in-law's body, which was hacked to pieces, was missing his fingers and ears. He died a martyr's death. The rebels who are hiding out in the mountains finance themselves by robbery, kidnapping and ambushing vehicles. People are afraid to go out after dark, even here in Tabuk." Pastor Teckney continued rather breathlessly with the tragic tale, as if wanting to get it off his chest as fast as possible.

"They hate Christians, and we have heard reports that Pastors have been murdered in the northern parts of

Kalinga Apayao Province. It is because I fear for your lives that I tell you these things. Even if you penetrated as far as Tulgao, it is doubtful if we could interpret for you. None of us have been there, so we do not know what dialect they speak." We listened quietly and intently as this godly man spoke. We could sense the traumatic effect that the barbarous death of his brother-in-law had on him, and how he could not bear the thought of a repetition. We cannot even begin to imagine the devastating grief that he must have borne in bringing home a hacked up body with missing parts, for burial. I sensed that he was close to tears, and that he had said enough to get his point over.

One could have heard a pin drop, as everyone's minds were preoccupied with their own personal thoughts. I broke the silence by saying, "I think that those who feel called of God to continue with our mission to the mountains should seek God's leading and direction. We must hear from God individually on this issue." I excused myself to go and pray.

Behind the house, I found a hammock slung between two palm trees which was well positioned in a shady spot. Lying back in the hammock I meditated on the things the Pastor had just told us. Everything around me was so peaceful and serene. Looking above I saw the fronds of the palms silhouetted against a cloudless pale blue sky. Nothing stirred to spoil the tranquility of the moment, and I felt perfect peace in my heart, that peace of God that passes all understanding. In the peace and tranquility that surrounded me, I found it hard to imagine that the people in this area were too terrified to leave their homes after dark. It was hard to believe that barbarous murders, robberies, kidnapping, and the ambushing of vehicles was going on in these remote places.

"Lord, I find it hard to believe that you would want us

to abandon the planned mission to the mountains, but I will submit my will to your leading and direction. Please reveal your will to me in this situation. Should we carry on as planned, or back out?"

The voice of God's Spirit spoke within me.

"There is no time to waste, and you have no reason to delay."

I was in complete peace, and no longer had any doubt. The mission to the mountain tribes would go ahead as planned. Betty's voice broke the silence. "There you are, I have been looking all over for you. I was beginning to think that you had been kidnapped by the headhunters."

"You should not say things like that, Betty."

"I sure am glad that God has not called me to go further than Tabuk. Have you made your decision?"

"No, God made the decision for me. We will go ahead as planned."

Walking back into the house accompanied by Betty, I said to the team, "Have you heard from God?"

"We prayed and asked the Lord to talk directly to you. We will abide by His leading through you."

The word of the Lord to me was, "There is no time to waste, and you have no reason for delay." Pastor Teckney rose from his chair and warmly shook my hand, "Be assured that we will faithfully pray for your safety, and that the mission will bear even more fruit than the last trip."

Turning to Pastor Padua I said, "Have you any doubts Pastor?"

"None. I submit my will to the leading of the Lord."

We were planning a visit to two villages near to Tabuk, before Betty left to return to San Fernando and her responsibilities at the mission there.

A hired jeepney carried us to our destination only thirty minutes drive from Tabuk. The driver was making a big issue out of the fact that he would not return for us after dark. This verified Pastor Teckney's words. "People are afraid to go out after dark, even in this area." My companions told him not to worry about us, as there was a Christian family in Epil who would give us lodgings. The jeep came to a standstill and we piled out. "We have to walk from here, but it's not far," the Pastor reassured Betty.

Pointing across the rice paddies he said, "Look, you can see Epil from here."

And there it was. A cluster of nepa dwelling houses on a sort of island surrounded by a sea of rice paddies. The straw roofs, at this distance looking like boats that had been moored together for mutual shelter.

There were no roads, not even a track into the village. The only approach was to walk on the narrow mud dykes which were approximately a foot wide, that separated the rice paddies.

"You mean we have to walk on these narrow dykes," exclaimed Betty.

She was a big lady, with a big heart full of love, but she also had a big tummy that made it difficult to view her feet from a standing position. Navigating one's way across the rice paddy dykes was a bit of a balancing act, and one had to watch one's step. We had gone halfway across the sea of rice paddies when I was stopped in my tracks by a loud cry. Turning to look behind, I saw dear Betty land on her back in the rice paddy with her feet in the air. It was a soft watery landing so she was not hurt, and in her usual manner she made a joke out of her circumstances.

Betty handled the local conditions extremely well and learned to take a bath Filipino mountain style. She was well padded, and coped with sleeping on the bamboo floor, without too much grumbling. I was the preacher at the evening meeting, and Betty was blessed to see the Lord confirming the preaching of the gospel with signs following.

Children with fevers were healed through faith in Christ's name. Within thirty minutes their temperatures returned to normal. The following morning we headed back across the rice paddies to meet with our driver, who had promised to return for us early next morning. To our great relief Betty made it back over the rice paddies without incident. She was such a kind, loving soul, but had the unfortunate manner of saying things, which seemed to make trouble for her. I gave her a gentle loving rebuke on more than one occasion. "Betty, please guard your tongue. The word says, "We get what we believe in our hearts and speak with our mouths."

We were once again on the road headed towards Sukbbot. Upon arrival Betty desperately needed to relieve herself. She had held on not wanting to use the toilet facilities at Epil. The toilet consisted of pieces of bamboo fixed together which formed a wall of privacy. I knew what to expect, but it was a completely new experience for my companion.

Within the bamboo walls was a deep pit dug out of the ground, which was full of maggots and all sorts of weird creepy crawly things. The air within the walls was alive with flying buzzing bluebottles, flies, mosquitos and other flying insects that I could not name. She took one look inside the bamboo walls and quickly retreated, holding her throat as if she was about to vomit.

The situation was desperate so she just had to get on with it. What happened next was like the worst nightmare anyone could experience. One had to balance on two bamboo boards, which were laid across the top of the pit. I was waiting only a short distance away, because I also needed to do what she was doing. Suddenly, I heard the sound of cracking wood. The noise gave way to a resounding crash. The bamboo boards had snapped under Betty's weight. Betty was shouting and screaming hysterically. "Help me! Help! Get me out of here! Help me God!" She was at the bottom of the pit, almost waist deep in maggots, worms, and untold numbers of weird slugs and creepy crawlies. The air around her head was thick with buzzing flying insects. I rushed to her aid, grabbed her outstretched hands, and tried with every ounce of energy I could muster, to get her out of that despicable hole. It was impossible. I could not lift her weight, and she could not help herself, as she could not get a foot hold. Her feet simply slipped and slithered in the slimy mess. "Betty, I will have to go for help."

As I left her and fled away to get help, the sound of her terrified shrieks and cries followed me. I rushed down the path way as fast as my feet would carry me, screaming, "Pastor! Pastor, the boards broke, Betty is in the pit with the maggots, and she can't get out." Every one instantly dropped what they were doing and headed for the "comfort room" to help Betty. I was first back on the scene and all was quiet, there was not a sound coming from the pit. "O God, she must have fainted," I thought. Looking down into the pit I could see the top of her head, she was still in a standing position. "Betty, are you all right down there?"

"Yes, I am praying to God, and asking Him to get me out of all these maggots and things before they start feasting on my flesh." Her imagination was at work as usual, but I was amazed that she was perfectly calm and in control of her terrible dilemma. Four men arrived to help hoist her out of the pit., It seemed an impossible task. At one point when she was nearing the top her foothold slipped and she disappeared back into the hole, almost taking her rescuers with her. Then a Filipino remedy was quickly implemented. The men tied a lasso knot in a rope, and threw it down to her. She placed it round her waist, and the entire manpower of the village got on the end of the rope, and slowly but surely she was hoisted up out of that despicable hole.

After she had thoroughly washed and changed her clothes, she said to me, "When you left to get help, I thought I would lose my mind, I was screaming and screaming, totally out of control. Then the peace of God came upon me, that peace that is difficult to explain. It simply flooded my being and calmed me down. God was with me, and with Him by your side you can cope with anything, even being stuck down a dung hole with thousands of maggots, worms, grubs and things with a dozen legs." I gave her a big hug. She had a special grace whereby she always made a resilient come back.

Another precious handmaiden of the Lord was the Pastor at Sukbot. I could not help but be impressed with Pastor Carmen's faithfulness. She never complained about the deprivation of the conditions under which she worked. Her concern was for the spiritual welfare of the people. God had called and anointed her to lead and teach them under His guidance. She had heard that we were definitely going back into the mountains and said to me, "You will be the only woman in your company, I have been praying and I believe the Lord wants me to be your companion." I was deeply touched by her willingness to come. She, more than most, would appreciate the dangers and the discomforts of living in the mountains, but I wanted to be sure that she had considered it carefully. So I said, "Pastor Teckney strongly advised us to stay away from the mountains of Kalinga, have you faced up to the fact that we may not come back alive."

Her reply was positive and final, "My life is in God's

hands. The fact that I am still alive is a miracle of God. The Lord miraculously intervened and saved my life." Carmen went on to tell me a remarkable almost unbelievable story, "I was leading the congregation in praise and worship, singing in the Spirit, and my eyes were closed. I did not see him come in, I did not hear him, I knew nothing until I was viciously grabbed by the hair of my head. Opening my eyes, I was shocked to see a man who was stinking of alcohol with a bolo in his right hand, raised in the air, ready to strike me"

"What is a bolo?"

"A bolo is a long heavy sharp knife. From the end of the handle to the tip of the blade is about eighteen inches in length. The blade is about four inches wide tapering to a point. It is used for cutting open hard coconut shells, and chopping up fire wood. The intruder's face was twisted and contorted with hate, and he pulled me towards him by my hair. The bolo was raised above his head ready to strike me. He brought it down with all his force on my neck, then on my arm and finally across my back. He struck me with all his strength, with three successive blows. God was with me. The bolo was sharp enough to slice my head clean off my shoulders. I never felt a thing, my neck, and arm and back were neither cut nor marked. It was an amazing miracle. There was not one mark on my body.

He was dumbfounded and amazed. He looked into my eyes with a look of absolute incredibility, dropped the bolo and fled out of the church." Pastor Carmen and her congregation fell on their faces before God and worshipped Him for the incredible miracle. With tears of thanksgiving they thanked God and praised Him. Carmen's body would have been lying on the floor a dead beheaded corpse, with an amputated arm, and her back sliced in two parts if God's mighty miraculous intervension had not occurred. When she overcame the shock of the incident, Carmen took authority over the demons that were ruling the man, bound them, tied them up in spiritual chains and commanded them to loose their hold of him, through faith in the all powerful name of the Lord Jesus Christ. Carmen continued, "The congregation never left the church that day, we prayed, praised, fasted and worshipped and interceded in the spirit, for the young man's salvation."

Later that week Carmen received a written message from the assailant. Would the woman pastor be willing to talk with him? His name was Eduardo. She related his story to me as follows. "He was born in the Northern regions in the headhunting tribal area, high in the mountains. His father was an alcoholic, and at an early age young Eduardo acquired a liking for the local rice wine, and often joined his father in his drinking bouts. His father became very aggressive and argumentative when drunk, and one night a quarrel developed into a fight. Eduardo's father came at him with a bolo. In self defence he grabbed this bolo to defend himself. With one swipe of the bolo he had beheaded his father. When he realized what he had done, he took to his heels and ran away from home, and wandered from village to village and finally settled in Sukbut.

He was unable to live with the hideous memory of seeing his father's head lying on the ground separated from its body. He regularly drank strong alcohol, to try and blot out the recurring nightmares that plagued his sleep. He rapidly became an alcoholic. He told me what had motivated him to kill me." The night before he attacked her, he was under the influence of strong drink and a voice spoke to him and said, "Take your bolo and go and kill the preacher woman." He had struck her hard enough to swipe her head clean off her neck, cut off her arm and put a great gash in her back. When he saw that she was standing in front of him unhurt, he knew that he was involved with a power that was far greater than him, or the voice that had spoken to him.

As he was confessing his sins, the Holy Ghost was working in his heart showing him God's amazing grace and forgiveness. He was a broken man, who fell on his knees in front of her, and through tears of repentance begged Pastor Carmen to forgive him. She assured him, not only of her forgiveness but of the Lord's forgiveness for the death of his father. He started coming to church regularly, and grew in the knowledge of God and was born of God's Spirit.

Eduardo was born in the mountainous regions of Kalinga and knew the dialect in the particular area that we were planning to visit. The place that Pastor Teckney said would be impossibe to evangelise, as no one knew their dialect. She was sure that Eduardo would be willing to return to his native tribe with our team, and be my interpreter. God works in amazing ways. Moses murdered an Egyptian but later became a great man of faith. This gave Eduardo faith to believe that God would also use him for his glory.

We eventually made it back to Tabuk after a successful mission at Sukbut. Betty thankfully had no bad effects from her dip in the maggot pit, but had quite a testimony to share when she returned to her home base. We put her on a bus bound for San Fernando and waved her goodbye, with her promise to pray that we would have a safe and successful mission into the mountains. The time had come to make final preparations for the next trip into the mountains of Kalinga Apayao.

Chapter Seventeen

Sumadel was very similar to another Stone Age village, which we had visited during my last trip in these perilous mountains. The gospel had penetrated this village, which was one of the stiffest uphill routes we had tackled. As we left the wooded area and emerged on the edge of the tree line, we were exposed to the full force of the tropical sun. The glare was dazzling, and I rummaged in my bag and found my sunglasses which I needed to protect my eyes from the glare. Then I covered my head with my big brimmed floppy straw hat to guard against sunstroke. We could now look over the glorious panorama of range upon range of mountainous beauty. From our position we could see the plateau from which we had just come. I simply stood and surveyed the majestic scenery. It was an amazing sight which spoke of the majesty and glory our Great Creator.

The village itself was amazing. The four hundred homes were packed together like sardines in a can, for mutual protection against headhunters. There were now more than one hundred Christians in Sumadel. Previously every home in this remote mountain village had its idols and superstitious charms and objects, and shrines where they worshipped their false gods. By the grace of God, paganism was in retreat before the gospel of grace, and it showed in the fact that cleanliness was so important to the people, and the wearing of clothes. They were taught from the scriptures that sex before marriage was not a Christian practice, and were taught the importance of keeping ones self sexually pure, for the right God ordained partner. How it thrilled my heart to see that God's word was bearing fruit in their lives. The importance of learning to read and write was an on going project with both adults and children, and a pre-school was already in progress. Pastor William had done a marvellous work in educating them through the scriptures. One of his favorite expressions was, "Learn to read so that you can get to know God through the Bible."

Every day through the preaching of the word, the Lord added more believers to His body. Before our departure, the new converts were baptized by full immersion in obedience to the word of the Lord, "Believe and be baptized." I also expounded God's word concerning the Lord's Table, and they entered into Covenant relationship with God, knowing that all their needs were freely provided in the atonement of Christ Jesus. It was a great joy to see them receive the word with child like faith. There were no barriers of unbelief through worldly brain washing, as is sadly the case in the more modern world.

I truly needed God's grace and power for strength to endure living in the mountain provinces, and to fulfill the planned mission. I was glad to eat the "bread of life" at the Communion Table, which maintained health, strength and sustained my life in such primitive conditions. I came into a new understanding of the scripture, "The spirit is willing but the flesh is weak." The hike up to this Stone Age village had been a long and arduous, hot, uphill hike, that had drained and sapped my physical strength. The change of water which was probably polluted, a diet of boiled rice and lack of sleep were taking their toll on my weak flesh.

It was impossible to get a decent nights sleep in a village where the houses practically touched each other. The houses were made of bamboo with straw roofs, and the sound of snoring indicated that your neighbour had drifted into the tranquility of sleep, wonderful sleep. Sumadel was geared for a very early start every morning. As the night curtain was drawn to reveal the light of a brand new day. All round the village the crowing of the cocks sang out their praises in a perfectly ordered relay. An alarm clock was totally unnecessary. The breaking of every new day had its own particular routine, first the cocks would begin their morning chorus, the dogs started barking, and the pigs would be snorting around followed by a trail of piglets with their high pitched squeals. Then the babies would start crying, demanding their mother's attention for the first suckle of the day. The bamboo walls and open windows shut nothing out. The continuous thump, thump, thump of the mortars pounding the rice to separate the chaff from the grain, informed everyone that the village was wide awake and functioning.

I was burning the candle at both ends. In the heat of the day we hiked to outlying settlements, ministered the word and prayed for the sick. We also conducted evening meetings in our host village. I was no sooner asleep than I was being woken up with the noise of the morning routine, which began with first light every morning. Pastor Carmen was an angel, truly a precious gift from God. She discerned my needs and understood that I needed help in mundane things such as washing clothes. She carried my washing to the creek, brought it back duly washed and laid it out in the sunshine to dry, along with her own clothes. When I was too weak to walk all the way to the creek, she got the men to carry water for me, so that I could wash in a basin in our room. She had a true pastor's heart and demonstrated the servant hood and humility of the Lord she loved and served. How I thanked God for her.

Chapter Eighteen

My God given subject for the evening meeting was, "The power of the Holy Ghost, in the life of a believer." Every day new believers were being born into God's Kingdom, and the forces of darkness were loosing ground. The brethren in this primitive Stone Age community were growing in the knowledge of God's word, but I was beginning to wilt. Arduous hikes through mountain ranges in tropical heat, trying to sleep on hard bamboo floors, living on a diet of boiled rice and what ever was laid in front of me sapped my strength. Preaching on a regular daily basis, casting out devils and praying for the sick, were all taking their toll on me. I was also aware of the spiritual forces that were opposing me. Oppressing demons were draining me of all physical strength, to the extent that I had no energy to fight back. I felt so exhausted and weak, that I thought my reason was going. How could I carry on? I felt as though I would lose my mind, and could not cope with the situation any more.

Falling to my knees, through lack of strength to remain on my feet, I realized that I had reached my end, and was unable to continue. I desperately needed divine intervention. I was too weak to pray, too weak to use my God given authority, too weak to do anything to help myself. When I was at my weakest point, the power of God's Spirit took over. The Holy Ghost literally took my voice and began to intercede on my behalf. I was aware that 'God in me', was interceding for me in the language of His Spirit. I do not know how long this miraculous intercession of God's Spirit continued. It could have been one minute or thirty minutes. All that I was aware of was God's power at work within, praying through me in tongues. During that time of intercession, God's power was renewing, restoring and strengthening my physical and mental frailty. Suddenly, I knew the battle had been fought and won. I had an inner knowledge that I would be able to continue with the mission, and finish the course. Hallelujah! God's grace and power was sufficient for me.

Using the testimony of the events of that day, I gave God all the glory for strengthening, renewing and healing me of total and utter exhaustion. My testimony amongst the people revealed to the congregation, the power of God's Spirit in the life of a believer. The entire village must have heard the intercession of the Holy Ghost through me, earlier that day. Now I was standing before them, strong and healthy and ready to face what ever lay ahead. Truly, the Holy Ghost is our comforter, enabler, teacher, guide, and intercessor. God's anointing was powerful in the meeting, which concluded with the majority of the congregation being baptised by the Holy Ghost, evidenced by praying in tongues, as God's Spirit gave them utterance. They had been endued with Holy Ghost power which fully equipped them to be Disciples of Christ. They were now in a position whereby they could obey the great commission, and reach out to other tribes in their vicinity. They had the power to preach the gospel, pray in tongues, cast out devils and heal the sick. By God's grace and power, I had accomplished His will and purpose amongst His people in Sumadel.

It was time to move on to Eduardo's home village higher in the mountainous region of Kalinga. He was a bit apprehensive about facing his family, because of the death of his father, but at the meeting he had been baptized with the Holy Ghost, evidenced by speaking in tongues. I was in no doubt that God's power, in him, would enable him to face whatever challenges lay ahead.

The following day we retraced our steps down from Sumadel, towards the valley below. In the cool stillness of early morning, we struck a good pace downhill and across the first mountain range. Within three hours we had reached the first plateau. The rice had been harvested, so we were not restricted to walking on the dykes between the rice paddies. Walking along the rice stubble was much faster than balancing on the dykes. An hour later we were facing the slopes of the next range. Eduardo said, "We must climb this mountain there is no way round it." With his finger he pointed to where a path zig -zagged through the trees and over the bare summit. It was going to be a long arduous, hot, hike. Reaching out to the Lord in prayer, I said, "Thank you, Lord, I know I can make it by your strength and enabling power."

It turned out to be a very irregular rocky track. Sometimes we had to squeeze along narrow ledges, with a deep drop into the valley below. I was never good with heights, and had to conquer the fear of falling. One misplaced footstep would mean hurtling down into the deep ravine. In other places, we had to jump over great cracks. Earth tremors and the power and force during the rainy season, of the heavy rains, caused great cracks in the rocky mountain. Sometimes the cracks were narrow and easy to jump, at other places the gaps were too wide to jump over. We had to do a Filipino remedy, and make a bridge, by placing a piece of wood over the gorge. It took unwavering faith, to step onto an old branch that had fallen from a nearby tree, knowing that a great ravine lay below.

Finally after what seemed like a day, we reached the summit. Eduardo was pointing his finger towards the top of the next range, "O my God!" I exclaimed when the realisation hit me. We had another mountain to climb, our destination sat at the top of the next range. There was still a long way to go, and after seven hours on the march, Carmen and I were struggling to keep up with the men. Pastor Padua and Eduardo were anxious that we reach our destination in daylight, as the route was much too difficult and dangerous for travelling in the dark. They pressed on at a pace that neither Carmen nor I could match. Looking at Carmen I thought, "She is so small," her height only reached my shoulder, but she was pressing on with God given determination. With head down I followed her example. I tried to ignore my aching muscles, which had jumped over ravines, scrambled up bare faced rock, balanced on shaky branches, crossed a valley and climbed one mountain, only to face another.

The muscles in my back and legs became so weak that my steps became shaky and uncoordinated, I simply could not go on, and had to stop. The consequences of not being able to carry on, and being stuck on this remote mountain, were too desperate to contemplate. Collapsing in a heap on the barren ground I mused, "This is headhunting territory. If I do not get up and carry on, I will surely loose my head, or my fingers or my ears, and maybe end up hacked to pieces." I immediately banished such thoughts from my mind. I must not give in to a spirit of fear. Pastor Carmen came and sat with me, and rested her weary aching muscles. "We will have to keep going, otherwise these headhunters will have an easy catch," I said to Carmen. We had reached the point of desperation, when one either laughs or cries. We looked into each others eyes, knowing that we could only carry on with divine intervention. Instead of bursting into tears of desperation, we spontaneously erupted into laughter. The men turned round when they heard our laughter, and saw that we were sitting in a crumpled heap on the ground. At first they thought we were crying. When they realized that we were in fits of laughter, they started laughing with relief. The mountain echoed back our laughter. The laughter resounded from mountain to mountain throughout the ranges. It was indeed a strange and uncanny experience, to hear the continuous sound of laughter resounding throughout the picturesque mountain range, far above us.

For what seemed to be minutes, we sat and listened to the sound of our laughter echoing back at us, and then we could hear the men's masculine laughter, as ours faded away. The sound was so infectious, that I put my hand to my mouth, to stop the sound of further laughter exploding from my lips. I began to wish that the noise of laughter resounding around the mountains would stop. Up until that point we had walked quietly, not wanting to be spotted by rebels or headhunters. Now the mountains echoed our presence to everyone throughout the mountain range. A new urgency came upon me and I prayed, "Lord God, we must keep going, please by the power of your Spirit renew, restore and strengthen our weak muscles and bodies, we ask it in the name of our Lord Jesus Christ." We all held hands and prayed in tongues, and I actually felt God's power surge through my body, and the trembling in my legs ceased, and my muscles stopped aching. "I felt as if a bolt of lightening went through me." said Carmen, and I knew that she had also experienced God's healing. restoring touch. We were on our feet again with uplifted hearts, and a new urgency to press on.

The sun by this time was high in the sky, and the heat of the day was upon us. We were soaked in our own perspiration, and our clothes clung to our bodies. Suddenly I heard a familiar sound, and my ears pricked up. Was I hearing the sound of running water, or was it wishful thinking? We all stopped, and looked in the same direction, then brother Oplaye took to his heels, and we followed in his tracks. It was a wonderful sight to see. He was kneeling before a little spring, and water was gushing out of a crack in the rock. He was splashing his face with cool, clear water. He then filled his plastic water bottle and drank, replenishing his body fluid, which had been lost in the sweat and exertion of an eight hour mountainous climb.

The sight of the water gushing out of the rock, reminded me of Moses at the rock in Horeb, and Christ who is the rock of our salvation. It was a reminder to me that we were on a God ordained mission, and that Jesus was watching over our every step. He was interceding for our success, and the souls that would come to Him through our witness. I exclaimed, "Praise the Lord, He is in control." To which my companions shouted a hearty, Amen!" Amen! Amen! Amen, cried the voice of the echoing mountain range. It was wonderful to feel the cool water on my face, and drink the water from the rock, which was cold and crystal clear. No doubt, tribes higher up the mountains were bathing their skin diseased bodies in the same water. "Thank you Lord, you have promised, if we drink any deadly thing it will not harm us. I bless and sanctify the water I have just drunk in your name."

Feeling refreshed and restored once again, we pressed on towards the second summit of the climb. "We will reach my mother's home in the daylight, if we continue at this pace," said brother Eduardo. The baggage boys did a great job, heading out in front, longing to reach our destination, and lay down their baggage burdens and rest. Finally the journey's end was in sight. According to Eduardo, we had been in full view of their lookouts for the past hour, and I began to wonder what kind of reception committee would be waiting for us. Eduardo and Oplaye took the lead, waving and smiling as we approached the village, and our company followed our leaders' example. We were greeted with the scene we had grown to expect.

Bare- breasted women with babies slung over their backs, naked children running around over the rocky surface in bare-feet. It always amazed me that their little feet were not cut and bleeding. Very young teenage girls were heavily pregnant or carrying a baby in a sling. The men wore only g-strings, and the majority were marked with many a tattoo, which they believed revealed their strength and masculinity. In my eyes it made them look fearsome and unapproachable.

Being of a different coloured skin, I was once again the centre of attraction, and people were appearing from every direction to take a look at this rare sight. Tangled hair and lice, dirty faces and mattered eyes, running noses, and sores running with pus from infected mosquito bites, no longer affected me. I was there in that remote mountain village, because God loved these people. Jesus gave His life to save them from the curse of disease, poverty and damnation, and I was there to give them the message of God's amazing grace and love for lost sinners.

There was not an armed man in sight, and everyone was friendly and curious. The men speaking with Eduardo and Oplaye, looked as though they were getting excited. Oplaye as well as Eduardo could understand their dialect and translated for me. "This is a very special occasion. No stranger, except uninvited headhunters from the surrounding areas have ever visited them before." They had a visitor who was a white woman, and it was an occasion for a celebration. They wanted to show their appreciation to their gods, for bringing this white woman to their community. Their celebration would take the form of sacrificing a piglet as a thank offering to their gods. They would summon up the spirits of their gods, by banging their sacred gongs, and performing their victory war dance.

We found ourselves in a very delicate situation. The last thing we wanted to do was offend the people. Suddenly the warning that God gave me on the plane, was brought to my mind.

"Behold I send an angel before you, to keep you in the way, and to bring you into the places which I have prepared. Thou shall not bow down to their gods, nor serve them, nor do after their works: but you will utterly overthrow them, and break down their images. You will serve the Lord your God, and I will take sickness away from the midst of them."(Exodus 23: 24 – 25)

I could not go along with this pagan ceremony, whereby they would be calling up demons. They did not understand that the spirits of their gods were demons. It was a very sensitive situation, which required Godly wisdom. I relayed my thoughts to Oplaye, and prayed that God would give him the right words to speak to the Chief without causing offence. He told me later what he had said, "The white woman has travelled a great distance in one of the flying machines which you see in the sky. She has especially come to tell the mountain people about the one and only true living God, who heals the sick without asking for sacrifices. If you kill and sacrifice to your gods, she will go away to the next place, and you will not hear what she has to tell you." The Chief walked over to me, and stood only a foot away, we were face to face, and he was looking directly into my eyes. I held his stare not daring to blink. I had to show him that I was strong in the Lord my God, that had brought me to such a place as this.

His eyes left mine and he surveyed me from head to foot, and back to my eyes. As our eyes met for the second time, I held out my hand, and he backed away from me. Turning to Oplaye, who I guessed was about the same age as the Chief, I held out my hand to him, which he immediately took. We shook hands with happy smiles. Oplaye then extended his hand to the Chief. The Chief got the message, as they shook hands with beaming smiles. Once again I extended my hand to the Chief, this time he grabbed it so hard, that I thought he would break my fingers. In spite of the pain he was inflicting to my hand with his vice like grip, I managed to smile back at him. We had started a new tradition, and the Chief started to shake hands with our entire company. His subjects followed suit, and soon everyone was shaking hands with beaming smiles.

The Chief then spoke to Oplaye, and Eduardo interpreted, "As this white woman has travelled such a long distance in one of the flying machines, we will hear what she has to say." He walked away, and beckoned us to follow him. He came to an open area between the native built houses and said, "The white woman can speak here this evening and we will listen."

Eduardo introduced us to his family. His mother hugged him with tears streaming down her face. "We thought that the headhunters took you away, the night they beheaded your father." It was believed that the headhunters had beheaded his father, the truth of the situation was under the blood of Jesus. We were all so hungry. Our stomachs were thinking that the headhunters had already got our heads. Within a short time, Eduardo's mother was serving us boiled rice and a local vegetable, on a banana leaf which served as a plate. We sat down and ate, looking out over the most beautiful, magnificent mountain vistas I had ever seen. The children were still inspecting me from a safe distance, when I looked back at them, they giggled with embarrassment. Carmen said, "Do you think I should try and teach them a chorus?" I nodded my head saying, "If you have the strength and energy, carry on." She began to gather the children together and was soon strumming on her guitar, which caught their full attention. She could not speak their dialect, so decided to teach them a chorus in English. I was amazed at how quickly they memorised the words, and were soon doing the actions, although they did not understand what they were singing.

A burning torch lit the appointed meeting area. I think it was twigs and branches tied together, which were fitted onto a bamboo pole. The moment had come, the Chief was sitting cross-legged on the ground facing me, and his subjects were in neat rows behind him. It was the enabling power of God's Spirit, which had brought us to this remote mountain top. After a nine hour hike up two mountains, I needed God's power to face the Chief and his subjects, and conduct the meeting. God would once again prove that which is impossible to our natural reasoning, is possible with Him.

For a moment I was lost for words, not knowing where to begin, as realization hit me with fresh force. My audience had never even heard the name of Jesus Christ. Yet they knew that sickness came from the power of the devil. Eduardo told us on the way up the side of the first mountain, that the people gave sacrifices to the red devil if they were sick. The procedure was explained to us as follows. If there was sickness in a family, the head of the household would present the witchdoctor with a chicken or piglet, depending on the severity of the case. The sacrifice was bled to death to appease the red devil. The witchdoctor then conducted a special service, and called off the spirit of infirmity from the sick person, by plucking a hair out of their head. It worked! The sick person was temporarily healed. After a period of time, when the witchdoctor was hungry, the person became sick again, and the procedure was repeated.

The words started to pour from my mouth by the inspiration of the Holy Ghost, and Eduardo began to translate for me. It was then that I noticed men sitting in the shadows with rifles slung over their shoulders. Blotting the scene out from my mind, I shared the gospel, explaining that the One True living God, the Lord Jesus Christ, had given His body to be scourged, beaten and lashed to destroy the power of the red devil. The red devil and all devils, know that Jesus Christ defeated them. They also know that they must obey His name, which is the most powerful name in the heavens above, on earth and under the earth. The One True Living God, the Lord Jesus Christ then gave His sinless life as the "once for all" perfect sacrifice for their sins. Jesus loved us so very much that He died the cursed death of crucifixion, to set us free from sins power to damn us to eternal damnation.

The Law of Almighty God declared, "The wages of sin is death, without the shedding of holy blood, sin cannot be pardoned." Jesus Christ died, and was bled as our substitute, to pay the ransom payment for all our sins, and save us from paying the penalty for our own sins, in the terrible place called the lake of fire and brimstone. Jesus Christ was Almighty God, the One True Living God, who came from heaven to earth, and allowed Himself to be scourged, to break the red devil's power to inflict you with disease. He died the cursed agonizing death of crucifixion, to cancel out your sin record. He proved that He was no ordinary man. He proved that He was the Almighty God, by rising from death.

The Chief suddenly stood to his feet, and addressed me in a loud, angry voice. The interruption immediately threw me, and silenced me, and gave me such a shock that my heart started to hammer at twice its normal speed. The language barrier was such a draw back, with bated breath and hammering heart, I waited for Eduardo's interpretation. The Chief says, "It is impossible for anyone to rise from death, and is questioning your integrity." Opening my bible at Mathew chapter twenty eight, I addressed the Chief saying, "Sir, let me read the report of the resurrection of Jesus Christ from the Bible. God's own word will convince you that the One True Living God, most certainly did rise from death after three days." By the time Eduardo had concluded interpreting the entire chapter, the Chief had relaxed, much to my relief, and was once again sitting in his cross legged position, with his head in his hands. He was giving me the impression that it was hard for him to believe that anyone could rise from death.

I was beginning to wilt. All these events were taking place at the end of a nine hours hike in tropical heat, through the mountain ranges. I needed divine intervention again. The Holy Ghost spoke to my spirit, "Take authority over the principalities and powers, which are opposing the truth of my word." I began to pray in the power of the Holy Ghost, and Eduardo followed suit. I then addressed the principalities, powers, and rulers of darkness, "In the name of the Lord Jesus Christ, I bind all demons of darkness and evil powers, that are opposing the truth of God's word, in the minds of everyone under the sound of my voice. Heavenly Father, please dispatch your angels of light, to take these demonic forces to the waiting place, to await the final judgment and be cast into the lake of fire and brimstone." I yielded my voice to the Holy Ghost, and prayed until I felt strengthened and able to carry on.

Directly addressing the Chief I continued. "You and your subjects pray to your idol gods and give sacrifices to the red devil, but the healing only lasts for a short time. When the witchdoctor gets hungry, he demands another sacrifice." I realized the Holy Ghost was meeting with them on common ground. I had the Chief's attention. He was nodding his head in agreement. "When your subjects have no more livestock to give for sacrifices, the witchdoctor and the red devil, leaves the sick person to suffer and die. The red devil comes only to steal, kill and destroy. If you want to be blessed by the one true living God, you must be willing to destroy your false idol gods, and stop communicating with devils. The One true Holy God is a jealous God, who will not share His glory with false gods. An idol is a dead thing, it cannot hear or answer your prayers, idols are lifeless carved pieces of wood or clay." I was aware that voices were being raised in opposition.

As the clamour rose from the darkness all around, I could see the men with rifles slung over their shoulders, standing in the background. Brother Oplaye gave me an encouraging smile. I then determined, "If I am going to be shot down, I'll go down preaching." The moment of fear passed, and I continued to preach. Then a loud mouthed staggering drunk was waving his fist and shouting at me. He was removed from the scene with one word from the Chief. I pressed on, until the point came that talking had to cease, I needed to prove the One True Living God with a demonstration of His power. "If there are any sick children here, bring them to me now."

A baby with a very high fever was brought by her father, laying my hand on the child's head, I could feel the heat rising from the little body, "I address you spirit of fever, and command you to loose your hold of this child, instantly. Go, to the waiting place, to await the final judgment, obey the name of Jesus Christ." The baby cried out as the spirit of fever departed from her. I then prayed in Holy Ghost tongues. As I prayed in the power of God's Spirit, I believed that a miracle was being performed, and that the baby's temperature was returning to normal. A few moments later, the father was holding the baby out for people to touch. They could feel that the fever was gone, as the baby's temperature had miraculously dropped. Her forehead, and the back of the neck, felt cool and normal. The Chief inspected the child, and he had to agree that the fever had left the child.

A teenage girl was holding her jaw in agony with toothache. Laying my hand on her jaw, I rebuked the spirit of pain and commanded it to leave her in the name of Jesus Christ. After praying in tongues, I commanded the virus that was causing the decay to shrivel up and die, in the Lord's name. As I prayed in tongues, she raised both her hands in the air and began to speak in her native tongue. "What is she saying, I asked my interpreter? "Thank you God! Thank you God! No more pain!"

Then they brought a man with severe back pain for prayer, and I was told that he had made many sacrifices to the red devil, but the pain always came back. I asked Eduardo to interpret for me, as I spoke to the man, "If you will serve the One true God, and turn away from false idol gods, witchdoctors and giving offerings to devils, the pain will leave you and never return. But if you serve other gods, pray to idols, or sacrifice to devils, the pain will return." He replied, "I will serve Jesus Christ as my only God," I prayed for him in the usual manner, and he was instantly set free of all pain. He was stretching and bending and lifting his knees with great joy and relief.

All eyes were on me and I concluded the message by saying, "Jesus Christ, the One True Living God, has demonstrated his power and proved Himself in your sight. Now you must make your choice, if you choose Jesus Christ as your God, please come and stand by me." A holy hush descended on the crowd, I stood there not daring to say another word and waiting for a response. The Chief rose to his feet and walked towards me. I held out my hand and he clasped it in a warm handshake. When I looked up another five men were walking slowly in my direction, my eyes filled with tears, which overflowed with a thankful and joyful heart. These men were stepping out of the kingdom of darkness and death, into Christ's glorious kingdom of light and life. Hallelujah!

The mission was successfully accomplished by the grace and power of God. The other members of the team took over, and ensured that the men fully understood what they were doing. Carmen and I were tired beyond words, and settled down to sleep in the Chief's house. Even a bamboo floor was appreciated at the end of that amazing day.

Our plan was to be up before the first light of morning. We had to retrace our steps back down through the mountain ranges to keep a rendezvous with Jacob our driver. We were keen to be on time, so that those who had been praying for us would have no cause to be concerned for our safety. Pastor Padua woke us up at four thirty, before dawn. Pastor Carmen was preparing breakfast, which consisted of sweet potatoes cut into chips, which were boiling in a pot. The aroma of the local coffee beans stewing in another pot filled the air. As we ate, the Chief came to share with us his wonder at what had happened the previous night.

Eduardo interpreted so that I was able to understand, that nightlife in that mountain village was normally very wild and unpredictable. The men come home from a days work in the rice paddies, hot and thirsty and start drinking their home-brewed wine. Very often the drinking bouts end with quarrelling and drunken fights, cursing and shouting. It had become even worse since the MPA distributed rifles amongst the tribes people. The peace would be further broken with rifle shots. Worse still, if they got into a rage over gambling losses they would shoot at each other. He was therefore amazed at the peace that ruled in the village since we arrived. There was only one drunken man. Only the One True living God could be capable of accomplishing such a thing. Those who were healed remained healed, the baby was doing well, and the man whose back was healed, was full of the joy of the Lord. The girl, who was healed of the pain of toothache, was helping Pastor Carmen to prepare our meal. Eduardo decided to remain in his home province, and teach his people God's word, so that they would grow in Godly knowledge.

Chapter Nineteen

" A LAND OF CONTRASTS" said the poster at the
bus station, but I doubt if the writer had been
exposed to the rapid changes I was experiencing. The
previous night I had slept on the bamboo floor in a native
built nipa house with straw roof, and bathed in a mountain
stream. Now I was speeding in an express air conditioned
coach heading for Manila. Tonight I would sleep in a first
class hotel and sit down and enjoy a perfect *filet de boeuf* in a
very pleasant restaurant. The contrast was truly amazing.
The mountain villages I had previously visited might have
been on another planet. I decided to take three days
complete rest. The hotel was beautifully furnished with air
conditioning and a very comfortable bed. I had the luxury
of both a bathtub and shower. Climbing into the warm bath
full of bubbles, I wondered what my little friend who had
taught me to take a bath mountain style, would think of this
bath of warm water and bubbles. It was like being in
paradise, compared to the life style in the mountain regions
of Kalinga Apayao.

After three days of total rest I was invited to minister in
Manila Bible School, "It is Good Friday tomorrow, and I
would like you to accompany us on an outing. I would like
to hear your comments of the events that you will witness."
said Pastor Isaguirre. I thought I had seen it all, but I was in
for another shock.

The face walking in our direction framed with shoulder
length hair, looked grey with fatigue and pain. It belonged
to a Filipino man about twenty-five years of age. He had
started out very early from his village, on a walk of penance.

This was a normal religious ritual, which happened all over the Philippines, on Good Friday mornings. In his right hand he held a whip made of ten leather thongs, as he walked he beat his bare back. First over his left shoulder, and then over his right shoulder, his back was covered with red weals, dripping blood.

A very large crowd had gathered in the square in front of a church building, waiting for his arrival. Many others who preceded him, arrived at fifteen-minute intervals, and were also torturing themselves by flagellating. When they arrived in the square, they prostrated themselves face downwards, and presented their backs to be lashed by a man and a woman, parading around with whips in their hands. After ten lashes they crawled on their hands and knees into the church, prostrated themselves and were lashed by another man wearing a priests robe. Then they crawled up to the altar and worshipped the statue of a woman with a child in her arms, kissed her feet, then proceeded to bow before the many idols and kiss their cold, dead feet of stone. A choir, working in shifts, kept up a continuous wailing chant throughout the day.

The last man was the one for whom the crowd was waiting. He finally made it to the square and prostrated himself, offering his back to be lashed. I did notice that they were not lashing with much force. He then made his way into the church, and went through the expected ritual of kissing the cold feet of the statues. Three men dressed as Roman soldiers then dragged forward a heavy wooden cross, that looked blood stained. It was most probably paint, made to look like blood. The cross was placed flat on the pavement at the bottom of the church steps. The last man to be lightly lashed was dragged out of the church, and laid down on the wooden cross. They positioned his arms outstretched on the beams, and firmly secured both arms with wide blue bands, wrapping the bands around his arms, binding him to the beam. This was done so that his body weight would not hang on the nails. His feet were placed on a pedestal, fixed to the vertical beam. His legs were also bound to the beam, and tied in place. The eyes of the man being secured to the cross had my attention. They were unnatural, and rolling around in his head, as if he was in a daze or a stupor. I came to the conclusion that he was heavily drugged.

He was given something to drink, then a black veil was placed over his face. He was now the centre of attraction. A hammer and two six inch nails was held up for all to see. No indication was given either from the participants or the spectators of the monstrosity of this act. I personally was feeling quite sick. Would they actually drive the nails through his hands? I had to see for myself. The man with the hammer in his hand, very carefully placed the point of the nail in a special part of the right palm, he lifted the hammer and brought it down with a sickening thud, and the victim was nailed to the wood. He then moved to the other side, and very carefully positioned the point of the six inch nail in victims' left hand. Lifting the hammer, he brought it down again with great force. The victims' left hand was impaled to the wood. The drugged man neither cried out, nor jerked his body, but lay there motionless as if dead, throughout the ordeal.

The cross with its impaled victim was hoisted into an upright position, and hauled up to the roof of the church, where it was fixed with a rope and left. The impaled victim hung there for approximately one hour. He vainly believed that he was doing penance for his sins. According to the doctrine of his church, penance is a requirement that gives one favour with God, and reduces ones time of suffering in purgatory, after death.

The events that we witnessed were an abomination in God's sight. This unscriptural religious doctrine, sought to deny the full sufficiency of the death and atoning blood of Christ, as being the full ransom payment for the sins of the world. Christ's sacrificial death was not sufficient for the members of this particular religion. They had to do penance and suffer in purgatory, a place that does not exist as far as the scriptures are concerned. This particular religion also promotes idolatry, and causes its adherents to pray to dumb, blind, lifeless, idols. The worship of idols is forbidden by God, and was the downfall of the Jews.

The careful binding of the victim's arms to the cross beam, the provision of the pedestal, fixed to the main beam, together with the binding of his legs to the beam, ensured that the victim's body weight would not hang on the nails. Jesus Christ made no provision to prevent His body weight hanging on the nails as He was crucified. Neither did he have a pedestal to stand on. His feet were nailed to the tree. What we had witnessed was a mockery of Christ's sacrificial death. I was sickened by what I saw. The Pastor produced a loudhailer and I preached to the people, telling them that the events we had witnessed was a mockery of Christ's death, and an abomination in God's sight. An ambulance appeared as they started to bring down the man impaled to the cross, which would take him to the hospital to be treated.

I wanted to get away from the scene and pray for the confused and deceived Filipinos, who were blinded by false doctrine and religious demons. We prayed that their eyes would be opened to the truth of the gospel. God so loved the people of the Philippines, that he gave his only begotten Son, who laid down His sinless body to die the horrendous death of crucifixion, to pay the full penalty for the sins of the Filipinos, as well as the whole world. The event that we had witnessed, was also taking place in many other locations throughout the Philippines, and continues to be practiced as a religious tradition. Jesus did not say follow a religion, He said, "Follow me. I am the way, the life and the truth."

"What is your final comment on what you have witnessed today?" asked Pastor Issigarie. "It is an abomination in God's sight and positive rejection of the scriptural truth of the gospel of grace." was my reply.

"I wholeheartedly agree with you Sister Chapman, but I have been persecuted for speaking out against these evil, satanic religious traditions, that is why I wanted your opinion."

"Blessed are you when persecuted for righteousness sake. You are blessed brother."

I was beginning to understand that religion was Satan's great tool to deceive people, and draw them away from the true gospel of grace through faith, to a false gospel of works, penance, purgatory, and idolatry. The world is indeed saturated with an untold number of different religions. Religion is not the answer to finding peace with God. The grace of God and the Bible are the instruments that lead individuals into truth and eternal life in Christ Jesus. If the doctrine of the religion we were born into, contradicts the plain teaching of scripture, then we are told to "come out" of that religion, so that we do not remain partakers of her sins, and receive of her plagues. (Revelation 18:4)

It is not easy to forsake the religion we were born into, because one gets criticized and spoken against. Regardless, scripture admonishes us to be pleasers of God rather than man.

Chapter Twenty

At the end of the meeting a young man pleaded with me to go with him to pray for his friend. When we arrived the house was in darkness. My companion called out his friend's name, and a bare light bulb clicked into life. Stepping into the room I was faced by a young man whose face was twisted in pain. He seemed to be wearing an extraordinary garment. On closer inspection I saw that his legs were covered with layers of coconut fibre, bound by leather thongs. Glancing round, I noticed that the small dwelling house was devoid of furniture. A large picture was hanging on the wall, which dominated the room. I knew that the people believed this to be a picture of Jesus, but there were no cameras in Jesus day. Therefore no one knows what He looked like. In my opinion the painting was a horrible representation of our Lord. First of all it was a picture of a white man with blonde shoulder length hair, and big blue, doleful sad eyes. The true Jesus was a Jew. Most Jews are brown skinned, with brown eyes and black hair.

Pointing at the picture of a fake Jesus I asked, "Who is this man?"

"It is a portrait of Jesus!"

"It is a fake. Jesus was a Jew, and all Jews are brown skinned, with brown eyes and dark coloured hair, just like Filipinos."

At that point the young man's parents stepped into the room, and the Father spoke, "Will you repeat what you have just said." in an angry tone of voice.

"Yes Sir, that portrait is a fake. It is not a picture of Jesus

Christ. Jesus Christ was a Jew. He had brown eyes, and brown skin and black hair. This is a picture of a white man with blonde hair and blue eyes."

"Follow me!" said the father, as he retreated back into the room, where he and his wife had just come from. His voice continued to carry an annoyed angry tone, so I prayed quietly in tongues, as I followed them into the next and only other room in the house. Pointing to another big portrait that dominated the other room of their home, the Father said, "This is our beloved Mother Mary, who intercedes for us." I was looking at the picture of a white woman with blonde hair. She had blue eyes, and was dressed in a blue flowing gown. Hanging on the same nail that fixed the portrait to the wall, was a string of rosary beads.

I had to be very bold and uncompromising in my reply, "Sir, I must be candidly honest, this is not a portrait of the Virgin Mary. The true Virgin Mary was a Jewess. She had brown eyes, dark skin and black hair. This is another fake. Further more, Mary is not a mediator of the New Covenant, Jesus Christ alone is the mediator between God and sinners." I opened my Bible and read from 1Timothy 2:5.

"For there is one God, and one mediator between God and men, the man Christ Jesus."

The true Virgin Mary was highly favoured and blessed above all woman, because she was God's chosen virgin vessel to birth our Lord Jesus Christ into this world. Mary was the Mother of Jesus' humanity, but she was not the mother of our Lord's Divinity. Mary's instruction to us was:

"Whatsoever He (Jesus) saith unto you, do it" (John2: 5)

Nowhere in the Bible do we read that Mary gave guidance or instructions, except to say, that we must do whatsoever Jesus said. We should not pray to Mary or saints, neither should we pray directly to Jesus, the only way to get your prayers answered is to pray to the Father, in the name of Jesus Christ.

"In that day ye shall ask me nothing. Verily, verily I say unto you, whatsoever ye shall ask the Father in my name, He will give it you. (John16: 23)

The mother of the household then stretched up her hand, and picked the rosary beads from its hanging position on the nail. "We pray the rosary every morning, noon and evening, because it gives us armour against evil, it destroys vice, decreases sin, and it causes virtue and good works to flourish. The rosary prayers guarantee that we will not perish, but remain in God's grace and makes us worthy of eternal life. It delivers us from purgatory, and gives us a high degree of glory in heaven." I was quite dumbfounded by their beliefs, which were contrary to the plain teaching of scripture and said, "If Mary could do all those things through rosary prayers, why did Jesus have to suffer the pain and agony of the scourge and the horrendous death of crucifixion? Tell me, why are your rosary prayers not working for your son, who is living with such pain?" They gave me a blank stare, and were unable to give me an answer. Turning to the young man I said to him, "Why are you wearing coconut fibres on your legs?"

"I have great pain that comes from my feet up through my body and into my head, and my feet are icy- cold all the time. Our witchdoctor came and sacrificed, and bound my legs."

"When did the witch doctor do this?"

"Two weeks ago, but it is not any better." he replied. The family was prepared to listen, and I shared the true gospel of grace through faith as taught by our Lord. Turning to the father I asked him, "Please tell me what you have been taught concerning purgatory?"

"Purgatory is a place where the spirit and soul goes when a person dies. During our life time, we commit both venial and mortal sins."

"Excuse me Sir. Can you explain the difference between venial and mortal sins?"

"Venial sins are little sins that may be forgiven. Mortal sins are bad sins which one must suffer punishment for in torment of purgatory. Once a person has paid the full punishment for their mortal sins, their spirit and soul are released to heaven."

"Sir, I must tell you that the Bible does not mention the place you call purgatory, sin is sin in God's sight, there is no such thing as little sins or bad sins. This religious teaching denies the full sufficiency of the sacrificial death and holy redeeming blood of Jesus Christ. The sacrificial death and redeeming blood of Jesus Christ, cancelled out the sins of those who accept Jesus as their sin bearer and Saviour. This doctrine of purgatory is a lie. It is not true, because it carries no Biblical warranty.

But this man, (Christ) after he had offered one sacrifice for sin forever, sat down at the right hand of God. (Heb10: 12)

By the which we are sanctified through the offering of the body of Jesus Christ once and for all. (Heb 10: 10) And almost all things are by the law purged with blood; and without the shedding of blood there is no remission. (Heb 9:22)

Neither is there salvation in any other, for there is NONE other name under heaven given amongst men, whereby we must be saved. (Acts 4:12)

Scripture makes it perfectly clear that Jesus Christ is the door way into heaven. He is the way, the life and the truth. Religion cannot save anyone. The Blessed Virgin Mary cannot save anyone. Rosary prayers cannot save a lost sinner. The Bible teaches that there is a place called the lake of fire and brimstone. This is a place of eternal torment. There is no escape from this terrible, terrible place. It is the place where all sinners will pay the penalty for their own sin. The sin that will damn sinners to this terrible, terrible place of eternal torment will be their rejection of Jesus Christ, as the one and only true Saviour of sinners.

This dear family was sincere in their religious beliefs, and struggled with the fact that they were deceived by religious doctrines, that were not based in Biblical truth. My heart overflowed with love for them, and I went and embraced the mother and she started to weep, and between sobs she blurted out, "I have been deceived by religion all my life." I just held her in my arms and prayed in tongues, believing that the Holy Ghost was healing the hurt of being totally deceived. When her sobbing subsided, I said to her, "Are you ready to destroy these fake portraits, and rosary beads, and accept Jesus as your sin bearer and Saviour?" She turned and looked at her husband, and my eyes followed her glance, he was nodding his head.

I got down on my knees and invited the family to join me. I led them in a prayer of repentance and renunciation of their religious beliefs, and involvement with the witchdoctor, and they accepted Jesus as their Lord and Saviour. We then unbound the son's legs and removed the coconut fibres, and I laid hands on him and bound all demonic forces that were at work in the family, tied them up in spiritual chains rendering them powerless and ineffective in the name of the Lord Jesus Christ. The pain instantly left the young man, and he began to rub his feet with his hands. He was rubbing his feet because they were tingling, the feeling of life and warmth was returning to his feet. We tore the pictures off the walls, and collected all their religious objects such as crucifixes, crosses, and rosary beads, together with the witch doctors coconut fibres and burnt them. "Why is it necessary to destroy the crucifixes?" asked the Father.

"Jesus is not a dead Christ nailed to a cross. He rose from death, and is now seated at the right hand of the Father, forever making intercession for us." He nodded his head with understanding.

Arriving back at the Calamoing home I walked into a frightening scene. Connie, the Pastors wife, was laying face down on the floor, she moaned in pain as her husband turned her over. He looked up at me and said, "It is her heart, she is having another heart attack." Looking down at her, I saw that her face was contorted by the violent pain she was suffering. The six people in the room dropped to their knees on either side of her, and spontaneously began to pray in tongues. Laying my hand on her forehead, I commanded the demon of darkness that was attacking Connie, to desist in this foul attack instantly. "Loose your hold of her now. I tie you up in spiritual chains and render you powerless, in the name of the Lord Jesus Christ." She continued to lie on the floor, unable to move or speak. We continued to pray in the Spirit. After ten minutes of intercession we saw her face begin to change, the ashen colour was changing and her own colour was returning, the pain was subsiding, and she managed to give us a little smile.

As we prayed in the Holy Ghost, she slowly levered herself up into a sitting position, then slowly stood up, and walked to her bed aided by her husband. I asked her daughter to bring me bread and wine, the symbols of the Everlasting Covenant. I knew that Connie had suffered with a heart condition for some time. The enemy had her convinced, that all her hard work over the years had weakened her heart. Sitting down on the side of her bed, I said, "Sister Connie, the devil comes only to steal, kill and destroy. He has convinced you that you have a bad heart condition, which you are claiming and possessing as yours. The devil is a liar, you should not believe him, but believe God's word. By the Lord's stripes you were healed." At that point Elizabeth walked into the room carrying a tray with the bread and wine. I went on to explain that God has made an Everlasting Covenant with us, and that it was impossible for God to break His side of the Covenant Agreement.

We have to receive the benefits of the Covenant by faith, as we eat the bread and drink from the cup of the Covenant.

Physical healing is a free gift of the Covenant, provided for us through the stripes of Jesus. We have to eat and drink in faith, with no doubt or unbelief. She ate and drank with full understanding and faith, and I led her in a prayer to renounce her heart condition. The following day she was fully involved in her work as a mother, housewife and bible teacher. A few days later she came to me and said, "It is true. We get what we believe in our heart, and speak with our mouth. I believed I had a heart condition because of the doctor's report, and often spoke about my bad heart, but no longer. I am standing firm on my Covenant rights by faith, and have not even felt a twinge since I had Communion." I was glad that her faith was firmly rooted in God's word, and not in the fact that I had prayed for her.

Chapter Twenty One

Our mission took us to a leper coloney where twenty six thousand families lived together in a fenced off town. The stench of death and rotting flesh was almost unbearable. I was filled with dismay, even horror, as I looked upon human bodies that had been ravaged by leprosy. Some victims had no fingers. Their fingers had been eaten away. Others had been eaten up to the elbows. Some had no feet, just stumps where the limbs had rotted away. Others had no noses, only two black holes where the nose had once been.

It was horrific. Only Satan and his demons could be responsible for the pain and the disfigurment of these poor lepers. It was almost more than I could cope with, and I fought back tears trying not to show how horrified I was.

The whole atmosphere of the hospital where the worst cases of leprosy were being treated was profoundly sad. My heart was bursting with compassion for these people who were rocking to and fro in such pain and agony. Why would God allow such suffering? God gave us the Old Testament and used His chosen people the Jews to reveal why people suffer. As long as the Jews walked in obedience and faith in the terms of the Covenant, they lived in good health, peace and prosperity. When the Jews got into a state of unbelief and broke their side of the Covenant agreement by turning to false gods and worshipped dumb, blind, lifeless idols, they stepped out of God's blessing, and the curse of the law automatically worked against them. They suffered disease, poverty, famine and defeat. Many died a premature death or were exiled to slavery in Babylon.

The people who lived in this leper colony were all under the curse of the law. The sin of idolatry appeared to be the reason for such suffering and the desperate state of these poor lepers. As I walked into the entrance of the hospital, I was faced with a huge altar adorned with many different kinds of idols. The idols had been presented with many and varied kinds of offerings, flowers, sweets, trinkets, and other objects. My companions then led me into another large ward with about thirty beds lined up on either side. Everything seemed so unclean, even the rags they used as blankets, were filthy dirty. Every bed had a wooden bedside table which was adorned with religious objects and idols. Standing in the middle of the ward, I preached the gospel to the hearers and stressed the sin of idolatry. Some wanted to have a theological argument with me, and refused to hear that their sad state was a result of the sin of idolatry and praying to lifeless idols.

Others argued that their suffering leprosy was a penance for their sins. They were suffering in this life, and would therefore spend less time suffering in purgatory after death. I was amazed to see how false doctrine had blinded their understanding, and made them believe that their suffering was God's will for them. It was beyond their comprehension, that Jesus had endured the agony of the scourge, to set them free from the curse of the law. The majority said the prayer to accept Jesus as their Lord and Saviour. Sadly, it was religious ritual, with no true understanding or faith, in the word of God, which had been preached to them. They most definitely were not willing to destroy their idols. No one can walk in the blessings of God, and possess dumb idols and pray to blind, deaf, lifeless idols. Thousands of Jews were put to death in one day, because of their sin of worshipping a golden calf as their god. (Exodus 32: 27 – 28) Idolaters are headed towards the second death in the lake of fire and brimstone, as is revealed in Revelation 21:8.

However the visit to the leper colony was not a wasted effort, they all heard the truth and they will not be able to deny this on judgment day. The few who allow me to smash their idols and renounced idolatry were miraculously healed. One such case was a man who was in a small room on his own. My interpreter explained to me, that the man could not speak, because his vocal cords had been eaten away with the disease. He had the usual religious wall plaques and a statue, which he venerated and believed were his link to God. I read the first and second commandments from Exodus 20. I then shared the gospel of our Lord Jesus Christ to this poor leper, pointing out that the New Testament also teaches us to flee from the sin of idolatry.

I explained with the help of my interpreter, that healing is a free gift, given to us by God's grace, through Jesus sufferings on our behalf. I also explained that he could not serve two masters. He could not serve Christ and venerate idols. He had to make a choice between Christ Jesus and idols. I assured him if he chose to destroy his idols he would be healed. He was nodding his head and pointing at the plaques and idol, and then he pointed at me. I said, "Do you want me to destroy those religious objects?" He was nodding his head most positively, so I picked them up and dashed them on the concrete floor, and the cheap clay broke into pieces.

Laying hands on him I commanded the demons of disease to loose their hold on him. "You no longer have a legal hold over this man. He now belongs to Jesus Christ, and believes that Christ has redeemed him from the curse of the law." Then I prayed in the power of the Holy Ghost, believing that the healing power which Jesus' stripes released was healing, renewing and recreating his vocal cords. Turning to my interpreter I said, "Now tell him to say, "Jesus Christ is my Lord." He opened his mouth and said, "Jesus Christ is my Lord." His vocal cords were recreated by the power of the Holy Ghost in the name of Jesus Christ.

Tears spilled out of his eyes as he repeated the same words a second time. It was a miracle.

"You must utterly destroy their idols," On the plane, that was the commission the Lord had given me from His word. The majority did not realise that venerating statues, pictures and religious objects was separating them from God's loving care and divine protection. Every where I went God was opening my eyes, and revealing the consequences of idolatry. What we had witnessed at the leper colony was the horrific consequences of generations of idol worship.

Confounded are all they that serve graven images,

that boast themselves of their idols. (Psalm 97: 7)

God is a merciful, full of grace, love and forgiveness for all sinners, including idolaters, but He cannot violate his own word. All who continue to bow before, pray to and serve graven images cannot escape the curse of the law, which includes eternal torment in the lake of fire and brimstone.

"Keep yourselves from idols" (1John 5:21)

Printed in the United Kingdom
by Lightning Source UK Ltd.
134961UK00001B/46/P